LEADERSHIP UNBOUND

A PRIMER *for* LEADERS *and* ENTREPRENEURS

LEADERSHIP UNBOUND

A PRIMER *for* LEADERS *and* ENTREPRENEURS

by Lawrence W. Corbett *and* Jerre L. Stead

published by
Five Star Publications, Inc.
Chandler, AZ

Printed in the United States of America

Copyright © 2005 by Lawrence W. Corbett and Jerre L. Stead

Published by Five Star Publications, Inc.

Five Star Publications, Inc.
PO Box 6698
Chandler, AZ 85246-6698

Library of Congress Cataloging-in-Publication Data

Corbett, Lawrence W., 1943-
  Leadership unbound : a primer for leaders and entrepreneurs /
[by LawrenceW. Corbett and Jerre L. Stead].
     p. cm.
  ISBN 1-58985-010-6
  1. Leadership. 2. Management. I. Stead, Jerre L. II. Title.
  HD57.7.C669 2004
  658.4'092--dc22

                                        2004029413

PUBLISHER
Linda F. Radke, Five Star Publications, Inc.
Chandler, Arizona, www.FiveStarPublications.com

EDITOR
Carole V. Bartholomeaux, www.b-pr.com

BOOK DESIGN
Barbara Kordesh, bkordesh@insightbb.com

PHOTOGRAPHER
Rick Mueller

www.LeadershipUnbound.com

CONTENTS

About the Authors

Larry Corbett and Jerre Stead met in 1997 when the Steads moved to Scottsdale, Arizona. By that time Larry had been at Pinnacle Presbyterian Church for seven years. Through the Steads joining the church, the men became friends, and Jerre served on the governing body as an Elder. Larry was on a two-week study leave when the idea came to him that the two of them should write a book comparing success in the church and in business. He sent an e-mail to Jerre with the proposal for this book. Jerre liked the idea and they were off.

Larry brings to the book several years of experience as a pastor. A graduate of Muskingum College, New Concord, Ohio, and Pittsburgh Theological Seminary, Pittsburgh, Pennsylvania, he has a Doctor of Ministry degree from McCormick Theological Seminary, Chicago, Illinois. During his career, he has served six churches:

- Fox Chapel Presbyterian Church, Pittsburgh, Pennsylvania, as a student associate pastor.

- Fairmount Presbyterian Church, Cleveland Heights, Ohio, as an associate pastor in charge of teen and adult education.

- Lakeview Presbyterian Church, St. Petersburg, Florida, as pastor.

- Westminster Presbyterian Church, Phoenix, Arizona, as pastor.

- Valley Presbyterian Church, Scottsdale, Arizona, as associate pastor in charge of administration and congregational life.

- Pinnacle Presbyterian Church, Scottsdale, Arizona, as founding and, subsequently, senior pastor.

He brings to this narrative a unique outlook about starting a successful church in north Scottsdale, Arizona.

Jerre Stead brings many years as a CEO and board member of major corporations throughout the world. In his business acumen he brings an analysis of what makes a successful entrepreneurial venture.

A graduate of the University of Iowa with a degree in business administration and the Harvard University Advanced Management Program in Switzerland, Jerre spent 21 years at Honeywell, Inc. in various management positions in the United States and Europe.

In 1987 he was named president and chief operating officer of the Square D Company, a leading electrical distribution and factory automation manufacturer based in Palatine, Illinois, becoming chairman and chief executive officer in 1989.

Jerre was named chairman and chief executive officer at AT&T's Global Business Communications Systems. He was promoted to executive vice president of AT&T and chairman of AT&T Global Information Solutions (NCR Corporation.)

In January of 1995, Jerre became chairman and chief executive officer of the Legent Corporation, where he led a successful merger with Computer Associates.

He headed up Ingram Micro in 1996, where he continued to capitalize upon his longtime philosophy that people are an enterprise's only sustainable competitive advantage.

Jerre is on the board of directors of Armstrong World Industries, Conexant Systems, SoftBank eCommerce, TBG Groups, and Brightpoint, Inc. He previously served as chairman of the National Electronic Manufacturers Association and as chairman for the Center of Ethics and Values at Garrett Seminary at the Northwestern University Campus.

Acknowledgements

We are grateful to many people who have assisted us in the completion of this book. Many thanks to Don Gustafson, Dave McIntyre and Diane Dicioccio for their critical eye and helpful suggestions in reading early drafts. Larry's thanks as well to Hazel Smith, a family friend, who was encouraging in the early stages of the vision, and to each other, for respective insights, experiences, and optimism.

A special thank you to Michael Sullivan for his keen and helpful editorial suggestions.

Most of all Jerre and I are profoundly thankful to our "silent partners", Mary Joy Stead and Meredyth Corbett, who have always lived and acted on their faith convictions giving to us, our families, and the church the depths of their love, wisdom and personal presence.

Dedication

We dedicate the spirit of this book to the next generation of 21st century leaders, our grandchildren: Madeleine, Sydney, William, Samuel, Jenica, Joseph, Winston, Maria, and Nathan. May they be filled with the spirit of visionary leadership and entrepreneurial commitment.

1

THE PURSUIT OF ILLUMINATION

LARRY

Under the fluorescent rays of a ceiling lamp, my derma-
tologist examined my nearly bare body through her
magnifying lens, making sure my fair skin and blond
head hadn't sprouted any carcinomas. As she inspected,
she asked me where I was working.

I replied that the Presbytery of Grand Canyon,
Arizona, was exploring the possibility of developing a
new church in North Scottsdale on land they had purchased a few years earlier. Being an astute business-
woman as well as a physician, she asked me, "Who
needs it? Who wants it? How will it get started?"

I answered emphatically, "The folks in that area need
a church."

She didn't accept my answer. "Yes, but, if those folks
don't know they need it, how will you get it started?" A
physician by choice and an entrepreneur by nature, she

had jumped straight to the heart of the issue.

I asserted that the residents of the neighborhood didn't realize that they needed a church, but they would perceive that need through my efforts soon enough. Wealthy people, like anyone, could not flourish without the light of the Word—and a church to radiate it. I knew that living behind guarded-gate communities amid magnificent golf courses with architectural-magazine-cover homes didn't give them immunity from encountering family problems, death, despair, disease, and dysfunction. Gate transponders don't keep sin, suffering, and darkness out of one's life; indeed, the gates often seem to lock in the frustration and loneliness.

Though the sun was bright in Arizona in the spring of 1989, and though the budding North Scottsdale community enjoyed a high quality of life, still this community needed the Gospel. They needed the Word of hope and meaning. They weren't going to find enduring happiness in a world of consumer-driven, leisure-time activities. I was filled with a passion for success, and my achievement-driven type-A personality would propel this project forward. People's lives would be stronger, more informed, transformed, and balanced—by the living light of the gospel.

Along with my passion for success and personal achievement, however, was a secret anxiety: I did not wish to fail in this project! I spent many hours of discussion with colleagues about a theology of risk in the coming days. To what extent was I willing to risk failure? In two decades of Grand Canyon Presbytery practice, far more new church development projects failed than were successful. I did not wish to have the Pinnacle Presbyterian Church added to the litany of lost causes.

Failure was not in my vocabulary. Failure causes a shadow of anxiety and self-doubt, and I wanted this project to succeed.

How does one come to terms with the risk of failure?

- By doing one's homework, it reduces the risk considerably.

- By clear definition and vigilant communication of *the vision.*

- By understanding the real and perceived needs of one's community.

- By planning carefully. Solid planning and hope for the future are so closely related.

- By accepting one's personal and professional limits.

- By identifying, capturing and leveraging needed resources.

- By building in essential financial, creative, and environmental support.

- By moving forward in faith with steadfast determination while maintaining momentum.

- By facing and resolving issues quickly, before they grow into major stumbling blocks.

- By keeping an open mind and being flexible. There's more than one way to solve a problem—find solutions in the light of the overarching vision.

Having confronted such questions with two colleagues in ministry whose judgment I respected, and having come to terms with the possibility of failure being fairly small, we began—with a leap of faith.

My job was to lead the development of a vision for—and a commitment to—a Presbyterian Church at the corner of Pima and Happy Valley Roads. Under the auspices of Presbytery, I brought together a small group of people to form a steering committee. This group consisted of representatives of the nearby Presbyterian churches of Mountain View, Desert Hills, and Valley Presbyterian. Valley was the parent congregation where I was associate pastor. It was their financial and in-kind support that would be critical to the success of this project.

For several months the committee met weekly to fashion our dream, consider how to make it a reality, identify potential obstacles to its accomplishment, and determine what steps would have to be taken to bring this dream to fruition. We were building a vision and from it, a basic business plan.

This book provides a model for leaders who want to begin a successful enterprise, whether in business or the church, to guide to success. It discusses the steps from vision to reality and how the role of the leader changes as the business or organization grows.

JERRE

Larry has shown that he as a leader understands the power of vision driven by fact-focused need. I have always said facts are our friends. Whether facts feel good or make us uncomfortable, we welcome them because they can only help us. Success comes from understanding what our customers and our communities need, and creating a realistic vision and environment around delivering it. Does your vision fulfill real needs? What are the facts? What environment will help fill that need? What facts will shape the environment? I prefer *actionable* facts—ones that point to intelligent next steps to take.

I agree with Larry about the importance of light. I have written and said before that leaders must "shine the brightest light in the darkest corner." Leaders ask the right questions—the ones that need to be asked, especially the tough ones. The brighter the light, the better we see what we're doing—in our relationships, interactions, decisions and plans. Leaders openly welcome facts from every viable source. That's how better decisions are made. That's how our strategies and processes are shaped.

Use Faith, Facts and Focus to Create a Need-Meeting Community

LARRY

Being aware of the realities of holding church in a temporary location, the steering committee's discussions included choosing an acceptable place to meet. It couldn't be just any place, but somewhere that would be easily accessible to the potential members and near the presbytery-owned land where the future church buildings would be located. It would have to be physically attractive in a community where quality of appearance merits high value. Ideally, it would be available at times other than prime time on Sundays.

Meeting these criteria was not easy. Schools have historically provided cafeteria space for new church development, however, none were in the area. No mortuaries with chapel space were nearby. No other churches were within a five-mile radius except for a very small, privately-owned marriage chapel at the end of a dirt road behind a cowboy bar. Another group of would-be church starters had already tried using it—with weak results.

Striving to be creative, I connected with Doug Kruidenier, a land developer in the neighborhood, who had his offices in the middle of Troon Village, a high-end residential development. It was designed as a future clubhouse and was surrounded by tennis courts, a putting green, shuffleboard courts and a swimming pool. I wondered what the chances would be. Is this the right place for a church? It was a long shot, but I was determined to research every possibility; try every door.

After a lengthy discussion about the limited options, Doug offered the clubhouse to us rent-free as his contribution toward getting the new church off to a good start! Little did I realize how productive this interaction, this touch point would become!

Doug was more than helpful; he was a virtual lighthouse of facts and knowledge. He knew where to locate recent demographic studies commissioned by a local corporation that was just starting construction nearby—a new shopping center, anchored by a grocery store. Moreover, a second country club was being built. As if this wasn't enough, Doug had insight into the community's future infrastructure plans. He said there would be a new freeway that would draw residents into the area.

Best of all, Doug's facts were actionable—and he offered recommendations that were wise and business savvy. He advised me to decide at the beginning whether to build a megachurch or a suburban church. At the time, I told him we wanted to build a suburban church with about 1,500–2,000 members and not a megachurch. He knew influential landowners and small business owners in the area. They were projecting explosive growth over the next decade within a five to ten mile radius. When I saw those demographics I was convinced our timing was right.

As a first step, I gathered information about the community, its demographics and sociological essence. I got to know the area and its people.

The church post office box was located in a nearby corner plaza with art shops, tourists gathering spots, and a couple of restaurants. Each day, when checking the mail, I walked around the shops and introduced myself to the shopkeepers. My intent was to make them aware of the new church, which would soon be in their neighborhood. Yet I also wanted to learn more—to do the homework.

So I also used this time to ask specific questions about what they perceived as the needs in the community. Who were their local customers? How long had they lived here? What changes had they observed in the community since they had worked in these stores? Where did the children go to school? Where did parents work?

My objective was to make sure that they knew me and that a church would soon be in the neighborhood to serve them and their clients. I also gained their support in a public relations effort to spread the word.

If the local shop managers, clerks, and owners didn't know that a church was in the neighborhood when potential homeowners among the tourists ask about the availability of churches, the risk of failure is increased. If they did know, it was lowered. I intended to see that they knew about Pinnacle Presbyterian Church.

At the same time, I went to the many new community developments within a five-mile radius of the corner on which Presbytery owned property. Introducing myself to the sales persons in the model homes I'd tell them about the church and inquire about their needs. I enjoyed asking them to share the questions they were getting from potential home buyers that they were unable to answer positively. With patience, I learned that potential buyers inquired about nearby churches, school locations, preschools, and childcare. It was apparent that young families were moving into the neighborhood, from the West Coast, and specifically southern California. At the time this neighborhood seemed like a retirement community for persons fifty-five years or older, but it was changing, and rapidly.

Later, when the chapel was completed and we moved into it in 1994, many of these same realtors met in the chapel for their weekly sales gathering before going to view new homes on the market. I love that kind of synergy: the church was increasingly integrated with its local community.

In *Theology of Hope* by Jurgen Moltmann (Harper and Row, New York and Evanston, 1965, page 19), he observes that in much of the New Testament, Christian hope is directed towards that which is not yet visible. It is so closely interwoven with the beliefs held by the church. "In the contradiction between the word of promise and the experiential reality of suffering and death, faith takes its stand on hope. To believe does in fact mean to cross and transcend bounds, to be engaged in an exodus. Yet this happens in a way that does not suppress or skip the unpleasant realities. Death is real death, and decay is putrefying decay. Guilt remains guilt and suffering remains, even for the believer, a cry to which there is no ready-made answer. Faith does not overstep these realities into a heavenly utopia, does not dream itself into a reality of different kind."

Moltmann also tells us that hope alone may not drive good planning, but with good planning, hope is enflamed! The key is not to strive after things that have no place, but to strive after the things that have no place as yet, but can acquire one.

Careful planning therefore, called for identifying those "as yet things/places" as specifically as possible. Just as the new homeowners were filled with hopefulness about their new beginning in the area, so was I about a new church. My hope was fueled by extensive planning and close attention to details, which involved the Steering Committee.

After the Glen Moor Clubhouse was accepted as the meeting site, the logistics and processes which would accomplish our objectives were considered by the steering committee. Basic needs included, but were not limited to:

- Chairs for worship.

- Piano.

- Hymnbooks (we asked local churches for "hand-me-downs.")

- Pianist.

- Quality soloists.

- Childcare.

- Parking provisions.

- Ushers (internal and on the parking lot).

- Treasurer.

- Bank account.

- People to count the weekly offerings and deposit in the bank.

- Church school teachers.

- Refreshments, including a coffee pot.

- Tables, supplies, etc.

It was a thorough exercise in market and sales planning. However, planning was more than developing shopping lists. Plans for training people to serve in the church's opening weeks were carefully drawn. The steering committee became more than a decision-making body; it was now engaged in the hands-on training of volunteers.

We also realized that a small turnout could be demoralizing. We "strategized" to find ways to "salt" the congregation with people from Valley Presbyterian Church, the parent group, so it would feel and appear successful from the beginning. We didn't want newcomers to know that there were only three couples, with my wife and me as the first members.

Training those responsible for greeting, ushering, teaching, and hosting of meetings was very much oriented toward appropriate friendly hospitality. We wanted our congregation to be user friendly and feel as if they belonged. Fact-based studies of what influences persons to make a decision about uniting with a church indicate that people tend to follow their feelings and perceptions of a church. Those impressions are made in the first thirteen seconds after entering the building!

As I pondered whether such an instant evaluation was realistic, I thought of my own behavior: I choose television programs with my remote even faster! And in the car, my stations of choice were quickly established by the fingertip selection buttons. So such quick decisions were quite possible if not probable.

With this and more in mind, all of us focused on being and making friends. We were committed to becoming more open, friendly, and informative. We created an environment in which visitors would feel safe, secure, and welcome.

To provide a useful and supportive environment, we knew we'd need to make the church handicapped accessible. On another level, we had to make the church a psychologically "safe" environment for individuals to bring personal questions, strong faith, or even doubts for inquiry and discussion. We were faced with the challenge of proclaiming the gospel's clear "Word of Truth"—yet do so in an environment which also strongly encouraged open inquiry and risk-free discussion as people sought to grasp the powerful meaning in the fact-based faith and assertions of God's Word.

Clearly, the issue of risking failure emerged again— not just for me, but as a dynamic in the lives of each of our potential members.

Planning also included a commitment by the Steering Committee to an ongoing process of decision-making and change. We were determined to gather information and feedback from the worship attendees, evaluate the worship and programs, and make appropriate alterations along the way.

For instance, we had agreed that in establishing and planning the first worship service that this church should be a full-service church. We intended to offer a worship service with quality music, including special music and a church school during the worship service. We strove for the quality of worship to reflect that which we envisioned the worship would become a decade later.

It all worked except the church school, one of the most important aspects of a church's life! There were only three or four children, all preschool age, and the plans for a church school on the outdoor shuffleboard court outside the clubhouse, although carefully prepared, were undermined by distractions like hawks, cactus wrens, rattlesnakes, tennis players, and bicyclists. The Sunday dress codes, which the parents had assumed were in place, included black-patent-leather shoes, which were quickly scuffed on the asphalt shuffleboard courts. The children were attired in adorable Sunday clothes—when shorts and T-shirts with tennis shoes would well have served them better.

In short, we chose to move the Sunday School from the shuffleboard court to the local country club employee lounge. It was a move from a fresh-air setting to a smaller, smoky smelling room walled in by soft drink and candy machines. Still, the indoor space, even with its negative attributes, was preferable to the wide-open spaces and problems of the north Scottsdale desert shuffleboard court! And, we strongly encouraged casual attire.

The church nursery for babies and toddlers was also located in the nearby country club. There, employees enjoyed peeking in on the children, and the chef often prepared a special snack just for them.

Church School for adults was a simpler issue to resolve: we met in homes of members and in the local gated-community's clubhouses.

People Who Need People... Empower a Few to Engage Many

In the book of Exodus, Moses' father-in-law, Jethro, sees all that Moses is doing and offers him friendly advice, "What you are doing is not good. You will surely wear yourself out, both you and these people with you. For the task is too heavy for you; you cannot do it alone." (Old Testament, Exodus 18: 17–18) Although I was determined to be successful in this adventure I couldn't do it all by myself, not even with the wonderful committed support of my spouse. I was one of those "people who need people"—as the popular song goes.

It was soon clear that it was imperative to empower others in this project. Who should they be? How could I identify and engage them? What should they bring to the project? Why would they be interested? What was in it for them? These were all issues to be sorted out in providing effective leadership. In an effort to heed Jethro's advice, I carefully identified several additional

persons in a five-mile radius of the church's future location who could be helpful in the new church project.

The challenge—before answering any of the above
questions—was to communicate the vision to them and
engage their response to it. Sales and marketing were
in the lead!

I am blessed with an ability to deal with a wide vari-
ety of people from Hispanic yard workers in the neighborhood to Ph.D.s, entrepreneurs and CEOs. Previously,
I have served churches ranging from a "silk-stocking"
congregation where communion was served by men
dressed in tuxedos to an integrated one in a black,
southern ghetto with free-style worship. Relying on my
interest in people, what makes them tick, and how faith
plays a role in their lives, I began identifying persons to
assist in the project on a long-term basis.

Perhaps a key to understanding this personality trait
is an interest in listening to people and what concerns
them. It's fun to get folks to tell their story. Coupled with
this was our own family life which was in the midst of
intense psychological therapy with the multiple, diag-
nosed problems of an adopted child. I made no deliber-
ate effort to hide my own emotional pain, nor that of
our household as we underwent weekly family therapy. It
was not something which I easily discussed—nor tried to
use or manipulate in an inappropriate manner—but I
simply acknowledged to others that I understood the
extent of their suffering in listening to their problems.
This understanding came from the fact that I didn't cause
my child's mental disorders, couldn't control them, nor
change them—and that acknowledgment seemed to help
people in similar conditions with their life's problems as I
listened to individuals in the neighborhood.

Preaching was another personal skill that attracted people to the church. I prefer a style of preaching characterized by story telling, narrative, and an ability to build bridges between the scriptures and daily living. In spite of personal success for so many of the community residents there still seemed to have a hunger to hear the gospel in a fresh way.

Perhaps the biggest adjustment came with my personal disappointment that the church did not grow as rapidly in numbers of members as I had anticipated. The grim reality was that the guard gate at the entrance to the gated community was an intimidating obstacle to friendliness and openness!

A surprising thing occurred one Sunday when an elderly attendee with cataracts on both eyes drove his brand new car right through the wooden outstretched gate—somehow not noticing that the gate was lowered in its extended position. Fortunately, no one was injured, and his wife told me a couple of weeks later that it precipitated the surgery to remove the cataracts, which she had been encouraging him to do for several months. She loved it! Although it was a harmless, humorous event, it made me realize that the guard gate was not only a real barrier but a symbolic barrier to new church development as well.

Yet the great Pinnacle adventure continued. The local presbytery had indicated to me before the start of this project that they would perceive this to be a new church development "probe"—in other words, they had no money to commit to it, not much interest invested in it, and would not be surprised if it failed. A probe was a watered-down commitment by the presbytery, something less than enthusiastic.

In response, money was not an "M" word. We discussed the need for funds openly, and challenged ourselves to be responsive to the gospel, and to give of ourselves with gratitude to the development of the church and its mission. Perhaps it was my own need to be goal-oriented in this project, but the financial support of its mission came without insurmountable problems.

The upshot was that my commitment to it for the first year or so was also full of much ambivalence. In my secret inner heart I still wanted to be a pastor of a tall, steepled church and continued circulating my personal dossier in an effort to receive a new call in the Presbyterian Church USA relocation process. After interviewing with large congregational, pastor-nominating committees from New Jersey to California and several cities in between, I kept coming in second to the candidate of choice for the search teams. After being rejected nearly seven or eight times in the course of two years I began to consider whether I should be investing more energy and commitment in the Pinnacle project.

With the encouragement of my wife and a family friend, and with prayer and much thought, we decided to put our house on the market. I announced the following Sunday we would be moving into the community and that we were committed to this project. To my complete surprise the congregation broke out in applause! And to my further naiveté, many more people then signed to be included as charter members. We were required by the Presbytery to have a minimum of 100 persons in order to be chartered. In the spring of 1991 when we put our house on the market we had only 68 names on the list. Five months later in November we chartered with 109 persons! So much for the concept of a probe in new church development!

I realized that the potential charter members didn't want failure either. They wanted to be affiliated with a winner. They wanted to know that the project would succeed. They were individuals who had been successful in their own businesses and wanted to see that happen in the church as well. These people were experienced, empowered, and personally engaged in creating a need-meeting community—and they were seeing the very first fruits ripen before their eyes.

JERRE

It's important that a vision has the substance to stand the test of time, and the Pinnacle vision has had this from the start. Larry and his start-up team together created a vision and a plan which have stood the test of fifteen years of time.

A vision also needs to include a metric—a success measure. Larry and the Pinnacle core team agreed that the vision was about "creating a suburban church with 1,500–2,000 members." There are other ways to measure, but they did set that down and executed it step by step to make it happen. People often say "If you plan well, it will happen." The proof is in the execution: plan all you want to, but you then need to make it happen.

Another classic example from a business standpoint is AOL (America Online). In 1990, it was "a dot"—literally. Initially, Steve Case's brother told him that it would never happen, that he should forget it— go back and finish his education. Yet Steve had a vision—he said he believed there would be a good 10 million AOL users by the year 2000. He was a little off: they have 35 million. Think of that.

He tried to get me to be CEO in 1995, and I said no—for a lot of reasons. For one, I thought he needed to continue in that position, because the founder needs to live out the vision and stay personally engaged in making it happen. Today, Steve will tell you about the people he searched out and hired—and how they took on bigger and bigger pieces, and then came Richard Parsons, the fellow who's now president. That role has been critical and the business would never have reached its destination without him. These people were committed to execution—they saw the need and the vision that Steve was building on, and they believed.

That's like the initial team of individuals at Pinnacle, who saw the need, believed in Larry and were on board with the vision. I think it is so important to be able to set a vision out at the beginning, be strong enough to stick with it and demonstrate the strength of leadership. I'm not sure you can teach leadership; it comes with the genes. You can learn skills, yet you must have the personal DNA. It's important for people to know that natural leadership talent, once you've created the vision, is as critical as where you're going with it.

I think it was 1992 before AOL did its first IPO. It was only $18 million. Today I think the market is at $65 billion. At one time Steve Case said it was the biggest thing he could ever imagine—yet he knew he had to do that to realize the vision.

Steve also had to step up and manage human relationships. This was a challenge because Steve's an introvert. When you sit with him at breakfast for the first time, he will look up—occasionally. He knew this going into the project, so he went out and hired two incredible extroverts who could attract people on a day-to-day basis.

From the beginning, Steve said he wanted to be different, more people-oriented. This was the early '90s. Business was still pretty buttoned down. Yet he said "no" to ties and formal wear. "Come to work when you want to, leave when you want to." It was radical then, when you think about it now—especially anywhere near Washington, D.C.—where the corporate headquarters are, in northern Virginia. He believed people were ready for it. I'm sure he was, though he's probably a little beyond Generation X. Yet that was part of the excitement and differentiation he created back when things were just starting to roll. People didn't believe they would make it. It was so funny the day they announced the merger with Time Warner. There stood Jerry Levin not wearing a suit or a tie.

Without a doubt Steve had the instinct. It was fascinating to me. And as Larry said, he as a pastor lived the vision; he wore the robes and ministerial apparel. Yet he executed on the vision from the beginning as well, looking at the church start-up as a businessman. He knew the only way he was going to make it was to attract top grade people—and take a new and different approach, a very entrepreneurial, effective one.

Delivering on the Vision:
Creating Quality Customer Experiences

LARRY

We've also demanded a level of customer-focused excellence from the beginning. From the church's standpoint, it began with the quality of personal attention that I would give to my flock—plus my characteristic follow-up. From the first Sunday, people have said to me and reported to our staff: "I've signed those church friendship sheets for 30 years, but this is the first time anyone has ever called me." We fax to a volunteer phone caller the list of everyone who has put a check mark by "desiring more information" or "wanting information on joining the church." Within 24 hours of their visit, they are called and asked how the church can help.

We want to engage visitors from the community. We reach out and ask: "What questions do you have about us? How can we help you know more about Pinnacle Presbyterian Church?" Every active volunteer is a salesman for us. That one follow up contact has done more good than any other initiative. It's the personal attention that has brought more people back.

We regard it as a key part of our customer service. Other churches don't do it. People have said to me that if the minister called them, they thought he was looking for money. They'd never been called except when there was an evangelism campaign—indeed, no one received a call just from visiting a church. We would even like to go so far as to say we tried to create customer delight. It is not enough to have customer satisfaction, I wanted customer delight. This church does that. I think that's why we are so different. We are always externally focused—on the community, in the right way—on winning people by providing individual satisfaction and delight.

One other skill we've tried to develop is the capacity to attract successful professionals and leaders like Jerre Stead, who are able to grasp the vision and guide us in our execution. We thrive on competent and credible individuals whose experience, skills, and abilities drive us forward. They are able to roll up their sleeves and help make it happen.

JERRE

I always start any new project by surrounding myself with awesome people. Then I focus the first six months on meeting individually to discuss what exactly we are going to create, and how we are going to get there. Then, I practice what I call "loose/tight management"—which is "everything's going great so just keep out of the way." If things aren't going great, then I move in closer, get tight, teach them how to move forward—build momentum. That's the way I operate, whether the organization is small or large, or small growing to large, or large growing larger. I generate the leadership light, ask the right questions, and then give people an opportunity to engage.

I was thinking about all the churches we've belonged to. The one that came to mind first was the International Protestant Church in Brussels. That had about 40 CEOs in the congregation and yet they never made effective use of them. Think about that. What an opportunity to engage and apply professional leadership talent. Yet they didn't see the possibilities, and it never really happened. That's important to consider—and somehow we've got to get past our limited thinking and get it into our heads that these people have been placed here by more than chance, and offer a great deal if we engage them in the need-meeting activities of the church community.

LARRY

I have worked in churches all across the socio-economic map. My basic assumption has been that if you can touch the life of a CEO or a corporate leader, you have the possibility of touching thousands of human lives. CEOs contribute to multi-national decisions that can shape and transform communities on a global basis. Our potential impact in carrying the gospel forward is greater than we realize —working in a neighborhood church with a geographically defined outreach. Together and with the right spirit we can penetrate walls, transcend boundaries and affect vast networks of people— go places we've never envisioned and impact situations we never personally see.

That's my underlying assumption and that's why when anyone comes in here and I see the Bruce Albrights (Dayton Hudson), Joe Larsons (Sparta Brush), and Lew Lehrs (3M), I've got to try to get them involved right away.

JERRE

It has worked in organizations—I've seen it and done it. Identify and engage that critical talent level. We've got to build that in. At the end of the day, it is the same thing I always try to do because in organizations I penetrate as deeply as I can. In the first three months in a new organization I'll hold as many as 200 listening sessions—one on one, for two hours. It's always, "What are we doing right? What should we keep doing that we're doing well? Let's talk about ways to stop doing what we don't need to be doing." I do this to find out what is going on in the company and with customers, but mostly I do it for insight on where the talent is. Once you find the talent, you run with them. That has made a big difference. I now realize that we will have this book complete and released before we know the ultimate success of this church. Yet the ultimate measure of success is that someday, when you retire, you can see your work—your community, your team—keep getting better, growing more valuable.

To give parallels in business three wonderful people who have started companies on their own come to mind. These entrepreneurs, like Larry, have great success stories. I believe there are some parallels between profit-based enterprises and educational or religious organizations. The three business people are all very different folks from all over the country. They each had a vision, just as Larry had a vision in starting Pinnacle Presbyterian Church.

They are Bill Bartzak, President and CEO of MD Online; Scott Lambrecht, Founder of Golflogix; and

Lance Stuart, President of WorkWell Systems, Inc.

Six years ago Bill Bartzak saw the opportunity to electronically get rid of the millions of pages of paper that flow between patients, doctors, hospitals and insurance companies. He noted the great inefficiencies. Bill led his company to success way past the start-up phase as did Larry with Pinnacle Presbyterian.

Scott started Golflogix, Inc. just over four years ago. This company is unique because Scott has surrounded himself with some very talented people. He has purposely kept the organization small. His vision was very clear and simple: how do you make it more fun to play golf by using today's technology?

Lance Stuart, in California, started WorkWell Systems, Inc. His vision was to provide an environment that reduces the number of work-related injuries and to provide a healthier environment for workers around the world. He saw that work-injuries led to poor morale, lower productivity and higher medical, worker's compensation, legal, recruiting, training and administrative costs. He found a solution for businesses to significantly improve profitability by dramatically reducing work injuries and accelerating the return-to-work process.

In each case these entrepreneurs followed the same role model examples that Larry has laid out in chapter 1. First and most important each of them had a vision. To succeed, corporations or any organization need a vision, a mission, a set of values, objectives, and strategies to meet or exceed those objectives. Then, of course, they need a day-to-day plan supported by processes and quality improvement that gets the organization, no matter who they are, better and better in each case.

When Larry and these other three entrepreneurs started their organizations, they had a very clear vision of what they wanted to accomplish. Each of them thought through the risk of failure. They all considered carefully the question of how to get started. Organizations today often begin with a vision of how to make things simpler or better. Yet success comes not from vision alone, but from a set of accompanying values that will lead the organization to continual improvement. Each had a mission and plan that was as clear as a roadmap—so that they would meet or exceed specific milestones they had set.

Businesses today must be nimble, quick, and flexible. They must also be externally organized—focused on discovering and providing value for their customers. Churches and educational institutions are no exception. The ability to meet, understand, and anticipate customer needs is the critical piece of the formula for success in each of these organizations.

When I think of Bill Bartzak and his quest to solve the problem of inefficient, expensive, redundant, inaccurate, and cumbersome paper flow in the medical industry, I think of his vision. When I spoke with him at breakfast in northern Virginia more than six years ago, it was very clear that Bill was optimistic. He felt that with the software he and his team were creating, his company could change the industry in two to three years. Today is six years later, and they are actually changing the industry. Did it take longer than he anticipated? Yes. Was he tenacious? Did he deliver the product when it was needed? Yes and yes. Did he anticipate the customers' needs? Yes.

The marketing and sales initiative that Larry emphasized was one that Bill has executed as well as anyone I've ever seen in business or industry. His company, once a tiny firm started in New Jersey, provides productivity tools and network tools for companies all across the United States. It helps patients, doctors, hospitals, and insurance companies respond to needs more quickly and more cost effectively.

The other dimension to each man's vision is recognizing their strengths and surrounding themselves with outstanding people. Larry had a steering committee. Lance had a partner, Cory Christensen. Scott Lambrecht built a team who brought talents to create success. They also, therefore, recognize the limitations of their own skills, experiences, and capabilities. Just as Larry recognized the realities of what he could and could not do and "filled in" with great people to help him, each of these other entrepreneurs I refer to did the same.

Perhaps most importantly, each of them, starting with Larry, has created an environment of success, excitement, and hope for people. They have taken the vision and pushed it into a reality of action, day in and day out. Larry and the other three entrepreneurs all faced the risk of failure—the tremendous personal risk both from a compensation standpoint and a personal drive standpoint.

Larry pointed out at the beginning of this chapter how tough it was to get funding and support. Bill Bartzak went months with no salary. Scott Lambrecht also went months with no salary. Lance and Cory went a year without salary and put their personal money into the company to keep it alive. Larry went three years without any raise in compensation. Yet, in each case, they all had a very clear vision and mission. They all had a wonderful set of values to build their foundation on and a clear set of measurable objectives. Each and all of these people thrive today, and have earned rewards from both personal and professional standpoints.

As this book unfolds, we'll see that each of the four individuals discussed in this book have overcome very difficult challenges. They have succeeded and continued to push forward.

When I think of a successful business, I like to think of a pyramid. Vision is at the pinnacle. Vision is where you are headed, where you can reach out to the future, and work backwards from that future.

Under it is a clearly stated mission with a measurable road map of how to achieve the vision. Next are the values, which constitute the foundation and strength of every organization.

Then we establish objectives—three or four at most—measurable objectives, which drive the reward system to enhance the behavior in each of the organizations. Clearly, everyone wants to win. Having objectives which are measurable ensures that we can calibrate our energy and motion and achievement—and

know how much we're winning by how far we have
to go.

The organizational pyramid is tall—and we've just
covered the tip of it—vision. Next we'll move into
making sure we have processes in place to execute
on all that we aspire to become.

Planning Questions *A wise person once said that recognizing a problem is halfway to solving it. With that in mind, take a few minutes and enter your responses to these questions. Refer back to them in the weeks and months that follow.*

THE PURSUIT OF ILLUMINATION

Chapter One

1. Who needs your project/product? _____
   Who wants it?_____

2. How will it get started?_____

3. What do you perceive to be "failure"?_____
   How may failure of your enterprise impact your personal life (and that of your family)?_____
   How can you reduce the possibility of failure? Have you come to terms with the risk of failure? _____

4. Can you state your vision in three sentences or give a 30 second commercial?_____
   Does your vision fulfill real needs? _____
   What facts will shape the environment/your vision? _____
   _____

5. Careful planning is essential to success—are you good with detailed planning? _____
   If not, to whom will you look for assistance?_____
   When plans are developed have you included implementation? _____
   Who will do it? _____ How will it be done? _____
   _____
   Do you have a realistic deadline? _____
   How much will it cost? _____

6. Empower a few to engage many—who should they be? _____
   _____

How can you identify and engage them? _____

_____

What should they bring to the project?   _____
Why would they be interested? _____
What's in it for them?_____
How will you measure their achievements? _____

7. What concerns do people in your market have about you and your product?
   How can you encourage people to need your product/service? _____

   _____

   How can you create so much satisfaction they can't stay away?_____

   _____

   What are you doing right? _____
   What should you keep doing that you're doing well? _____
   What should you stop doing that doesn't need to be done? _____

   _____

8. What are your organizational values? _____
   How do your values and visions support each other?   _____
   Do you have three or four clear, measurable objectives? _____
   Have you identified rewards for their accomplishment?_____

   _____

   Have you developed strategies for meeting and exceeding your objectives?

   _____

2

Mission, Values, and Processes: This Church Means Business

LARRY

The gospel always carries with it a command to go into the world with the Good News – the life-changing Message. That's the core, compelling mission of any Christian organization, as it was for Pinnacle—and as it has been for me. Throughout my life I've thrived on the challenge of meeting people, listening to their stories, and sharing from the heart. Perhaps it's genetic, as people often observe that I'm a clone of my sociable, outgoing father.

Self-motivated, I am driven to excel and achieve. Whether it was high school sports or the college debate team, I wanted to do my best. Both parents instilled in me the old adage, "If you're going to do it, then do it right!" If there was something I couldn't do right, like

repair a car, my father would ask me to hold the flashlight. It is still part of family lore that if you need someone to hold the light, then please call Larry.

My parents always encouraged me to fulfill my
potential, and even at a young age, I became adept at
finding ways to make good things happen. I didn't seek
the spotlight, but I volunteered a lot, and made it my
mission to shape success for whatever organization I
joined. I grew up in a town so small it didn't even have
a stoplight, and was educated in a three-room school
until the seventh grade. With so few students, the
teacher knew us personally—and whether each of us
was actually working to achieve our potential.

Having a successful father and a wise mother was a
major advantage. In 1989, as I pondered each successive
step in creating a new Christian community, I drew
upon lessons from my ministerial experiences and the
helpful voices of my youth. I had made a career of
church leadership, but the Pinnacle challenge was something altogether different.

In this chapter, we share what we have learned about
what start-ups must do to be successful:

- Start with a clear vision for the future that stands
  the test of time and can be measurable.

- Understand the mission that serves as a road map
  to meeting or exceeding one's vision.

- Establish fundamental and critical values that
  provide the foundation of every decision made in
  an organization.

- Clearly define three or four objectives that are
  measurable and provide rewards for a winning
  team.

- Then develop strategies and road maps for meeting, or better yet, exceeding the objectives.

Once these tools are in place, and only then, should you approach people about who's funding.

JERRE

My wife, Mary Joy, and I have lived all over the world and belonged to 15 different church families. Church has always been a very important part of our lives together, ever since we started dating in high school. Our move to Scottsdale in September of 1996 was our last move. We had bought and rebuilt a wonderful home on the Desert Highlands golf course and were now ready to find our new church.

We have always church-shopped with each move, looking for an active congregation with a great staff that would provide us an opportunity to serve God and our community.

Since we had owned second homes in Scottsdale for many years we had attended several Methodist churches. Sherm Jones, who owned the home we bought, had suggested to us that we try the relatively new Pinnacle Presbyterian Church less than two miles from our house. We went there on our first Sunday, with the expectation that it would be the first stop in our continuing search for just the right Christian family.

After one service listening to Larry, feeling the wonderful friendship and warmth of the congregation, enjoying the choir and meeting new friends, we were ready to join at once. In all of our church activities we had never felt more comfortable then we did at Pinnacle. Larry was clearly a friendly, thoughtful and strong leader of a new and vibrant congregation. Looking back now seven years later we feel so blessed that God led us to this community and to this church!

Taking a Boundless Message to a World of Boundaries

Again, one of the theological assumptions which fueled my energy and vision was the concept that the gospel needed to be proclaimed to the community surrounding Pinnacle. I only hoped that the area residents could be persuaded to join. Again, earlier attempts by mainline denominations to begin a congregation in the North Scottsdale area had failed. An oversimplification is that they had been unable to gain the support of the community. What did Pinnacle Presbyterian Church have that would now elicit their support and not doom it like previous church development efforts? Would past history become a significant obstacle to an effective ministry? I was convinced it would be possible to overcome this negative attitude by establishing a clear and coherent growth process.

Since success was predicated upon community support, I started by contacting area Presbyterian churches within a ten-mile radius of the proposed new church location. Specifically, I asked their ruling boards (session) to appoint two people from their church to serve on the Pinnacle steering committee. Preferably these people would own homes in the Pinnacle Peak area. I fervently hoped that these people would become charter members of the congregation. Three congregations were pleased to assist, but the fourth, about seven miles away, was very unhappy about our endeavor. In the end, each church sent a husband and wife to be part of the steering committee.

The people selected for our steering committee were enthusiastic about starting a new church in the area. At that time, they had to drive at least ten miles to a grocery store or twelve miles to a shopping mall. Many commuted 20–25 miles each way to work. Valley Presbyterian Church had approximately 30 members living in the Pinnacle Peak neighborhood. The long commute to church became an issue for them.

The success of any project is related to knowing your target market, their typical behaviors, preferences and real needs. It wasn't as easy as saying, "Pinnacle Presbyterian Church will draw from a five mile radius of Pima and Happy Valley Roads." What quickly became a major issue was church boundaries. Typically, congregations in the Presbyterian Church, USA (PCUSA) are organized on a fast-food franchise model where there is one restaurant every five to ten miles. An alternative is to build a large regional church, which grows into a megachurch.

Another boundary concern was that we not encroach on any new development projects of another denomination. To handle this potential problem, twenty-five years earlier the greater Phoenix area churches formed an ecumenical organization called Interfaith Coalition on Ministry in the Southwest (ICOMS). It included representatives from Presbyterian, United Church of Christ, Brethren, Moravian, Methodist, and Lutheran hierarchies. The assumption among the participants in this coalition was that none of them would begin a new church project within a four to five mile radius (boundary) of any of the other participating ruling bodies without their cooperation and financial support. In effect, they would not compete against one another for new churches and recruit persons to unite with these new ICOMS churches but would cooperate in planning for new congregations, selecting a mutually agreed-upon site. They encouraged people from each of the denominational identities to unite with an ecumenically supported, new church project in their neighborhood.

For a couple of decades this covenant process seemed to work in the greater Phoenix area. But when Pinnacle Presbyterian Church began in 1989 the ICOMS agreement was coming apart. The multi-denominational commitment to it had waned, and the steering committee felt no compulsion to honor it at that time. In some ways this was not a problem because there was only one other new church and it appealed to the ranch-hand market.

Unfortunately, the Presbyterian Church seven miles away would have much preferred that our project did not start. They saw us as far too competitive and threatening to their ecclesiastical life and future. The issue at stake was related to the establishment and honoring of appropriate geographical boundaries for local congregations in order not to impede the growth of each of these churches by the development of a new one.

Indeed, I was to discover later that the grumbling church sent an elder to attend our services in order to find out what was going on. The underlying intent was to see how they could slow our progress and undermine us. As a noteworthy aside, the elder "scout" liked what she saw—and later joined our congregation.

In an effort to reassure the leaders of the nearby Presbyterian Church that it was not my intent to steal their members, I met with their interim pastor to discuss our mutual anxieties about the building of a new church. We acknowledged that we were friendly competitors in a nearby market. Our talk concluded with the following handshake agreement that we would:

- Avoid soliciting members away from one another.

- Refrain from marketing in new housing developments near the other's respective churches.

- Refrain from overlapping general mailings to zip codes which appeared to be seeking new members from common areas.

From that day forward this understanding appears to have held and has worked for both congregations.

JERRE

In this case, it was better to channel energies and limited resources toward cooperation rather than competition. For a young start-up, the top priority has to be building positive networks of upbeat, talented people who can attract and grow customer assets. When initial resources are so very limited, focus on the ability to understand and serve customers and communities better than anyone else. Getting tangled up in conflicts with other churches would not help us better serve our customers.

LARRY

Nevertheless, the issue of boundaries is an important one. The idea of geographical boundaries became too restrictive for churches in the last decade of the twentieth century. People started driving great distances when their destination gave them meaning. Families and individuals drove across town for a yoga class, to shop at their favorite mall, or to eat at a special restaurant. Little league practices can draw families from over ten miles away, three or four times a week. The same is true for churches. The yearning to meet spiritual needs will typically draw people beyond a five-mile geographical boundary.

A more tender issue is that of ethical boundaries in the development of a church. It is tempting to treat this boundary issue with avoidance, i.e., "If we don't identify it or discuss it then it'll go away." From the earliest conversations of the Pinnacle steering committee I firmly held that in everything we did at the new church we had two underlying premises. The first was to do everything with excellence. The second was to follow the golden rule of "Do unto others as you would have them do unto you." (New Testament, Matthew 7:12, Luke 6:30)

Consequently, the Golden Rule became an ethical norm for the mission and ministry of Pinnacle Presbyterian Church. The tension between the two competing congregations has eased to some extent because we discussed it early. We sought to treat other churches in the area in a manner with which we would like to be treated with regard to recruiting new members.

On a professional level, there are personal boundary issues that every pastor faces whether it is a new church development project or working in an established church. Nearly every day in a pastor's life, he or she is confronted with members of a congregation seeking moral guidance or a confidential listening ear as they seek to sort out the confusion they face with family relationships and personal choices. After this area of professional responsibility is established, the pastor then discovers that the same person is in a dinner group gathering for a social activity on Saturday night. In a social setting the pastor must not violate the ethical boundary of confidentiality and pastoral privilege even though it is a place where boundaries are very relaxed.

In Arizona, a behavioral health therapist would lose his or her license if caught socializing in such a manner with clients, but a pastor is placed in such a position routinely. A local church pastor must be able to use much personal discretion and discipline in moving back and forth between being a counselor, friend, dinner partner, and fund raiser—wearing multiple hats depending on the situation, crossing over boundaries with frequency and informed professional judgment.

The perceived theological boundaries for the new church came by way of my personal life and convictions. My inclination was to four basic tenets as a foundation for the project:

- Honor the great commandment of New Testament Jesus, "to love the Lord our God with all of our heart, soul, mind, and strength; and our neighbor as ourselves."

- Preach a gospel of grace, love, and forgiveness.

- Invite a personal response of gratitude and commitment from the hearers.

- Build a vigorous church education program.

With this framework in place, I began to work with the steering committee, which agreed to meet weekly beginning in March 1989. The target date for the first worship service was the first Sunday of October, that same year. We sought to simultaneously see the big picture as well as the up close and familiar one of all the details for starting a church. (See chapter 1)

Thinking, Planning and Acting in the Future Tense

Realizing the influences on a fledgling church would set the direction of the church for many future years, the steering committee invested time in creating a vision and determining what a church facility should look and feel like in the twenty-first century. What were the values and lessons of the past that we wanted to maintain in the future? What could be improved? We found ourselves going back even further as we determined that we valued the history of the nineteenth-century development of the church in the southwest and along the southern coast of California rooted in the missions of Father Kino. We also appreciated the ecclesiastical and architectural Mexican influence on present day New Mexico and Arizona churches. What had been successful in other places and why? What had failed?

In addition, we discussed the need to preserve the Sonoran Desert unique to this geographical region of the southwestern United States. This environmental concern was to be a major factor in the selection of an architect four years later. Preserving it was to be a financially costly issue later but one that has sustained the natural beauty of the desert and provided a sense of sanctuary beyond the newly constructed buildings.

It became evident that the big picture included a God-centered religious life where people could worship. The church would be a safe haven in which people could seek answers to their Biblical, spiritual, moral, and ethical questions without being judged, rejected, or deemed unimportant. This openness has sustained church growth in the first decade of our congregation's life.

We decided that the buildings on the church campus should give the feeling of a personal retreat/sanctuary to escape the hectic pace and lifestyle of the north Scottsdale area. Rather than the first building being the traditional fellowship hall, we wanted a sanctuary for worship. Being rooted in history and the desert environment we acknowledged that we were undertaking to build a church, both architecturally and organizationally, for the high-tech culture of the next one hundred years. Our big picture began to take shape through seeking to balance history, culture, the environment, and a gospel call to serve the future.

While we were setting the parameters of the future congregation, we also crossed some major traditional Presbyterian boundaries. The first is related to how a pastor is normally selected for a new church development. Usually a committee from Presbytery (district or diocese) interviews candidates and selects the minister. This person is parachuted into a new community without the benefit of having a support system in place to start a community-development project.

The Pinnacle project was different in that I was on the staff of another church in the Valley of the Sun and went to the Presbytery to ask permission to start a new church in the area. I knew people and resources that would help make this project a success. Valley Presbyterian Church became a parent congregation and offered support staff to do the secretarial necessities of bulletins, mailers, and correspondence. They sent members to assist with ushering and greeting. This congregation also pledged to support my new congregation and pay my salary over a three-year period. Without their loving help, the task would have been much more difficult.

There were many in the Presbytery council who had problems with this unconventional way of starting a church. The way it is traditionally set up, I believe, increases the risk of failure. Funds from the Presbytery of Grand Canyon bought the initial five acres here. They make the monthly payments on the land. What then happens is as soon as the church is chartered and declared a viable congregation, the remainder of the debt is transferred to the local church. A 100-member church struggles to raise money for a building and to get programs and the ministry going. Then, kapow, they are suddenly hit with a large debt and are expected to make payments on it. It overwhelms them! It puts them in a hole and in an untenable situation. It creates failures. In my judgment that is exactly why so many of our new church starts have failed. They've had this tremendous financial burden they couldn't handle, and they were so busy raising money that they weren't free to focus on community needs, strengthening the new church. Church folk of lesser vision and charity think: "That's not fair!" We were fortunate, though, because Valley was so supportive.

Creating and sustaining a safe, spiritual and Biblical comfort zone for the members also created tension with the denominational standards of the PCUSA. For instance, the denomination has identified so many different causes which the denomination supports with all of its diversity that a local congregation could have each Sunday identified as the XYZ day for the church. These causes are each worthy missions of the church, i.e., seminary support, small church growth, church education, children's day, and more, but they are diversionary concerns to a new church development. If a new church program sought to support each of these projects, the energy and financial support so necessary for the new church would be dissipated and cause its infant life to be snuffed out.

On a more theological level, the denomination has engaged in serious debate in recent years on ordination standards for its clergy, elders, and deacons. Such debate has caused great conflict and divisiveness across the nation in the PCUSA. I believed that such issues ought not to be a high priority in the early life of a church, but should not be ignored either. Therefore, we sought to answer questions which would routinely surface in new member classes, adult education classes, etc. I perceived that our local issues needed to be more focused on laying a foundation of openness, acceptance, and commitment of people to serving the local community through Pinnacle Presbyterian Church. When we had our foundation in place, then there would be room for controversy.

The Only "Supermodel" That's Beautiful Is the One You Create and Manage

---

JERRE

The lesson here that matches perfectly in the world of business is this: the leader has to understand the existing model for the extended enterprise and marketplace. I have to understand the boundaries that are in place, and then I make conscious decisions about how I am going to use or change them. A new business by nature will change the landscape of the marketplace. Boundaries can change, and do so all the time—yet the existing model is a snapshot of a present reality. For one, I believe the area of geographic boundaries is too restrictive. In a free market, customers and communities drive the placement of boundaries as their needs and preferences shift, not organizational police. So to create the new "supermodel" for your business operating environment, watch your customers and design a system that will meet them where they are with what they value.

It would be fun and helpful to readers to know how Larry personally thought through and worked out the challenge of so many boundaries. If you think about it, any organization needs to map out the real and future boundaries it sees—from the very beginning. It's important to do this as it helps to set expectations and create strategies that inspire—yet are also realistic.

From experience I know it takes a lot of intelligence and talented people to rethink, remodel and then execute those aspirations. At one company, we reconfigured the business model around customer-focused teams comprised of interdisciplinary professionals of varying functions. This broadened our dialogues with customers and strengthened our connections, while growing our collective insight into their business needs and issues. It made us more effective—and gave us an edge, knocking down old boundaries.

In any case, readers should feel free to question boundaries—and look at how boundaries could change in the coming months or years. It helps to know which boundaries to respect, and which to challenge.

LARRY

Another boundary we broke was meeting in a community clubhouse. No one had ever met in a real estate office before. Traditionally, new congregations either met in schools or funeral homes or community buildings.

The question is always a real one of how much freedom should a local franchise have in operating its business by stretching beyond the standards and norms established by the corporation? McDonald's is struggling because they are not meeting the new needs of the individual markets that they serve. McDonald's is relatively new. It has not (and may not) survive the challenges that come with change. The Presbyterian Church has survived for hundreds of years, but it too must evolve to survive and succeed. It must follow closely the needs of the communities in which it has a presence.

This will require new, adaptive strategies and re-learning processes, which are modeled to meet needs and improve the quality of life for people as circumstances change over time.

Adapt ASAP: Meet Changing Needs, Solve Real Problems or Disintegrate

JERRE

Two things are becoming apparent to me as we work through this process. The reason Larry is so successful is he did break the boundaries; and, if a church doesn't practice the out of the box thinking that Larry did, it's going to perish. I don't care if a church is Presbyterian, Methodist, or part of another mainline group—a lot of them operate in similar ways. Larry did a good job of screening and protecting the new church from vision-impaired Presbytery veterans. The flip side is if we don't start attacking real problems soon—and stop attacking young churches like Pinnacle—the denomination is just going to self-destruct.

The thrill of starting a new organization, setting a vision and acting to fulfill a mission is often quickly smothered by a lack of realistic processes in place. Start-ups can also have resource management issues, or lack of experience—thus not knowing what to focus on as they seek to execute plans and act on their mission. In each of the four cases that we mentioned in the last chapter, they set very clear boundaries and executed well.

In the world of business you would translate boundaries as "focus." Recognizing "what can be done and where we should best focus all of our energies" is fundamental. These fast growing firms were always looking externally, "outside-in" at their organizations. Helping customers be successful is a sure way to win.

Just as Larry said, the gospel needed to be proclaimed to the greater Pinnacle neighborhood. The three entrepreneurs: Bill Bartzak, President and CEO of MD On-Line; Scott Lambrecht of Golflogix; and Lance Stuart, President and CEO of WorkWell Systems have each said, in essence: "Our products, software, service offerings will help our customers accomplish what they want to do more quickly, more easily and more effectively."

Moreover, too many organizations have failed simply because they did not maintain the commitment to excellence necessary to attain their original set of objectives. They didn't spend their energies to perpetuate a healthy focus on the two or three things they could do better than anybody else. All too often as organizations grow, they lose sight of their vision and core capabilities. They try to do too much, be too much, and chase too many disparate opportunities. They fail to set specific, long-term goals and stay on a course to achieve those goals.

Larry drew examples in this chapter of things that could have resulted in loss of focus. He made sure that didn't happen. When he talked about making sure that we stayed focused as a congregation on building a foundation instead of becoming distracted by many, many other causes or the XYZ day for the church, he made sure that the boundaries, as previously defined, were clear from the outset. Keeping them clear helped the church be a truly wonderful success.

One of the reasons that Larry was successful in leading a church startup was that from the beginning and on an ongoing basis he listened very intensely to the needs of his community, his customers. Listening to customers and anticipating and meeting their needs through the filter of their vision is something that too many organizations forget to do each and every day.

Like Larry, Bill has converted his MD On-Line systems to meet the ever changing and ever more complex needs of medical requirements. Scott has a two-pronged customer focus. He has a product for the consumer as well as a product for the golf course businesses around the world. Golflogix has created a product and tools that help customers to make their golf game better and more fun either by buying it themselves as a consumer or using it on golf courses that have purchased Golflogix products.

WorkWell acquired a twenty-year old business that is the world's leader in work-injury prevention and rapid, safe return-to-work. Lance redirected its customer focus (and modified the service offering) from physical therapists to employers. He recognized that employers have the most to gain, the greatest ability to effect needed change and the greatest ability to pay for these services.

Over the years, I've told each and every organization that I've led that the only reason we're allowed to continue to be in business is that we provide customers with something that they need. We must do a better job than our competitors at meeting customer needs. As a reminder, I always communicated to my organizations that their paychecks were being paid by our customers.

When Larry started the church, he had a vision and a clear set of objectives and values. They were excellent in every way: personal attention for everybody, a community center on a campus that respects the desert, and wonderful music programs and opportunities. These objectives and values were formed for all people in the community, whether they were members of the congregation or not.

Finally, and a very important part of the focus was a wonderful church school as well as a preschool for the youth who will be the future leaders of our country.

If we look back to 14 years ago and then look forward, we can see that those four very key objectives have helped Larry accomplish a wonderful success in meeting a vision and now setting a vision for the future.

In every company I've been involved with over the years, we've listened to what the customer is saying about our products and services then tenaciously and aggressively scrambled to satisfy their needs. This creates success in a company, be it financial or in terms of market share. It is a personal success when members of the team can feel that he or she contributes to winning. As we said earlier, people want to win and need to win.

It is important to remember that successful businesses/ organizations do not set primary organization objectives like:

- Go public (IPO) in X years.

- Make $X profit.

They set primary objectives around "delighting" their customers better than the competition by offering superior services at a better value. Without achieving these primary objectives, financial objectives would not be attainable nor sustainable.

I've been through hundreds of educational, religious, profit, and nonprofit doors over the years. In just two or three minutes of walking through an area and talking to people I can tell if they have what it takes to be successful. I know if they are winning through working in pursuit of a great vision. In each case, where I could feel a great desire for success, I also saw the leader set an example role-model as no leader attempts or asks his or her team to do something that he or she wouldn't expect of themselves.

Keys to success in every organization come down to surrounding yourself with great people, staying externally focused, managing in and around boundaries and concentrating on two or three key objectives. Each of the organizations that I'm talking about has continually sought excellence by constantly listening, on a day-to-day basis, and learning about their customers' needs.

Start-ups don't want to be encumbered, or should not be encumbered, with too many rules, procedures, or policies. What they should have, though, is a clear set of objectives. We talked earlier about what helps everybody know the foundation of their values, where they are going, and how they will get there. Staying as nimble as possible and allowing people as much freedom as possible is critical. This is not irresponsible freedom in the sense of allowing people to go off and do whatever they wish. The right approach recognizes that people need freedom to meet or exceed their objectives, freedom to take responsibility, and freedom, if you will, to help each other be successful.

I always think of the three P's for each person: power, permission, and protection. They need power to meet or exceed their objectives and make the decisions they need to make to help customers be successful. Permission is about learning and making mistakes and to learn and grow at an ever-greater pace. Hopefully, they won't make the same mistakes over and over.

Finally, protection means working in an organization that understands how important it is to let people try new things. When a mistake is made, employees need protection to help them by providing the right priorities and allocating the right resources to correct the problem then move forward. If more organizations could sustain that kind of focus, just as the four entrepreneurs have done, they would remain nimble, while attracting and retaining critical people to do great things.

Externally-focused organizations must know and understand who their competition is and how they will react to organizational efforts. Just as Larry outlined the competition in his target market, each of the companies I've referred to in this book had to develop a clear understanding of their competitors' primary marketing focus. They also have had to understand what their organizations must do to meet or exceed customers' needs in a more powerful and successful manner than their competition.

Again, competition helps teams understand if they are winning or losing. Competition forces focus on customers. So understanding competition while staying focused or staying within the boundaries is a critical way to success. Larry has done what we see in successful businesses that really focus on their prime objectives.

This brings us to the next challenge. In Chapter Three we ask: "Who is paying?" This refers to where organizations go to find capital to fund the startup, whether it is a church or a business like those which we have cited. Before we address the "who's paying" issue, though, it's critical that we've made sure we've filled in the blanks in that pyramid we introduced in chapter one.

PLANNING QUESTIONS

MISSION, VALUES, AND PROCESSES: THIS CHURCH MEANS BUSINESS

Chapter Two

1. What must your start-up do to be successful? _____

2. Do you have a clear vision for the future that stands the test of time and can be measured? _____
Where will your company be two years from now? _____
_____
Where do you want it to be? _____
_____

3. Do you understand that your mission determines the road map to meeting and exceeding your vision? _____

4. Have you established fundamental and critical values that provide the foundation for every decision made in your organization?
_____
_____
_____

5. Success is related to knowing your target market. Do you know the demographics? _____
Typical behaviors of your target market? _____
Their preferences and real needs? _____

6. What are the important boundaries of your target market?
_____
Have you identified personal, corporate, and legal boundaries for your enterprise? _____
Do you have philosophical boundaries which will impact your enterprise?
_____
How do answers to these questions relate to your vision and purpose?
_____

7. What are the values and lessons from the past which you wish to maintain in the future? _____

What could be improved? _____

What has succeeded in other places, and why? _____

_____

What has failed in other places and why? _____

_____

Where are you going to get this feedback? _____

How? _____

8. Do you have a clear understanding of the existing model for your enterprise and marketplace? _____

How are you going to use the boundaries or change them? _____

_____

How might boundaries change in the future? _____

_____

Which boundaries will you respect and which ones may you challenge?

_____

9. How do you translate boundaries into focus? _____

_____

What can be done and where should you best focus all of your energy and resources? _____

Have you looked "outside-in" at your enterprise? _____

10. How will you listen to your customers to determine their needs? _____

_____

How will those needs be filtered through your vision? _____

_____

11. Start-ups don't want to be encumbered, or should not be encumbered, with too many rules, procedures or policies. How will you adapt your vision/ purpose/objectives through this assumption? _____

_____

_____

_____

3

WHO'S PLANNING, WHO'S PERFORMING—
AND WHO'S PAYING?

Sink, Swim or Walk on Desert

LARRY

Can anything on earth be more important and exciting
than developing a new community of believers? Isn't
this the great commission the church received from the
Master himself? Just think of it: the process in which
new Christian communities are conceived, nourished
and supported is the grand light-bringing vision of the
Redeemer, a transcendent "plan for the fullness of time"
to unite all things—highest priority of the great
Shepherd and Counselor. Knowing this, one would
think that large Christian denominations would focus
all of their energies and resources on this primary

mission, becoming subject matter experts, learning how to be agile, resourceful, creative and expert in the highly significant practice of bringing new church communities to flourish, blossom and grow. The overriding concern would be the magnificent art of church-building, with every church officer a master consultant at multiplying the ways a new community can be effectively developed and sustained. Ah, yes. If only that were the case!

On the contrary, among leading Christian institutions, this area is sorely lacking in shared expertise and consensual support. In Chapter Three we talk about the parameters: those you can negotiate and those you can't. Then we will move on to funding. The system for beginning a new Presbyterian church is typically a conflict-producing experience. It sets up a no-win situation between the Presbytery and the new congregation. A critical problem is that the denomination owns the property and assets while the local congregation functions as trustees for the property. Other mainline denominations function in the same manner. Legalities and hassles are numerous. It requires personal acrobatics to leap, race, and maneuver around the barriers and hurdles that denominational policies present.

Church members are usually unaware of this policy because most haven't served as officers on a local church board. As members of a congregation they are asked to make financial pledges and gifts toward the purchase of the property they will maintain, the construction of buildings and worship facilities their families will cherish and develop. As financial contributors, they feel ownership of the land, property, and facilities.

In fact, they are merely nominal trustees on behalf of the presbytery. How stunned and surprised they are to discover that after their planning, praying, and performing they have purchased property that does not belong to them—and never will! These practices virtually guarantee conflict, suspicion and resentment in the young community.

A second dynamic in this particular presbytery is its policy of shifting the payoff burden for remaining land debt to the local congregation at the moment it becomes chartered.

In 1984, Grand Canyon Presbytery paid $234,000 for a five-acre plot on Pima Road in north Scottsdale as a potential site for a new church development (NCD). The presbytery assumed monthly payments to the denomination for money it borrowed to purchase the site on the assumption that when the NCD congregation was chartered the monthly payments would then shift from the presbytery to the local congregation. And, indeed, this happened in December 1991, to the newly formed congregation of Pinnacle Presbyterian Church with 109 members. We were suddenly handed a relatively colossal mortgage with the corresponding handcuffs—significant monthly payments. There was no transition period, no adjustment, and no discussion.

This model for the financial support of new churches in the Presbyterian Church, USA, is fairly typical throughout the nation. Unfortunately, it becomes a significant financial burden on a new congregation of a hundred or so members (perhaps 50–60 regular financial donors at various levels). Remember: at this point in the congregation's natal life, the local church is faced with financial burdens that include but are not limited to:

• The organizing pastor's compensation package.

- Operating costs for a new congregation (rent, program costs, etc.)

- Construction of a first community worship facility.

Moreover, they are burdened with the additional monthly mortgage payments on the presbytery-owned land.

The other issue that created a conflict was the Presbytery of Grand Canyon's insistence that the organizing pastors not be compensated more than ten percent above presbytery minimum salary. This policy grew out of an effort to provide an equitable standard for the roughly thirty churches receiving financial aid from the presbytery, many of which were struggling to survive in their Hispanic and Native American missions. It seemed reasonable to adopt a policy of standardized compensation among the aid-receiving churches, including most NCD projects. Some of these NCD projects were in minority areas but most were in predominantly Anglo areas in the greater-Phoenix area or other urban areas of the presbytery including Prescott and Flagstaff, Arizona.

Historically, one or two large congregations in the presbytery have helped to "parent" an NCD project from a sense of local mission, but these financial gifts sometimes only prolong the new church's agony. The young church struggles to manage woefully inadequate funds as they seek a minister for a new church and its community. Indeed, over the last twenty-five years this Presbytery has started several NCD projects that have never grown to more than a hundred members—and were too often not viable.

I was determined to avoid this model for our NCD. I believed that such a model was unrealistic and destined for failure. The facts were on my side. Housing costs alone in a five to ten mile radius of the presbytery's north Scottsdale church site were among some of the highest real estate prices in the country. This made it impossible for an organizing pastor to live within the church's community—unless he or she was independently wealthy and willing to personally bear the cost. Moreover, it is poor practice to start a new church development without residing in the community and visible interaction with your fellow members at the stores and parks—even on morning jogs. I was neither wealthy nor ecclesiastically altruistic, but I was willing to work hard and creatively. I also believed strongly that there was a need for a Presbyterian church at this site, and that I was in a position to make it happen.

Before starting Pinnacle Presbyterian, I was an associate pastor at Valley Presbyterian Church, a 2,300-member congregation in Paradise Valley, about twenty miles away. I had seven years experience in that position, and had been blessed with a generous compensation package. Given the added workload and responsibilities, I didn't believe that it was appropriate to cut my compensation by more than $25,000 a year.

As an alternative to Presbytery funding, I initiated conversations with the pastor of Valley Presbyterian Church and its session to devise a plan for Valley to fund the new church. After securing their endorsement, I realized that this would prove to be not only exciting and challenging, but would have a higher likelihood of success.

After some conversations, we arrived at a plan with these components: I would remain on the staff of Valley Church for three years with a compensation package

that would decrease by one-third each year. We anticipated that the new church could assume responsibility
for an additional one-third each year. This formula
allowed me to be the organizing pastor as a member of
the Valley Church staff, keep my office there, and maintain my historical compensation rather than take a
severe income cut.

Second, Valley would designate $80,000 of its pledge
to a Major Mission Fund, a denominational drive at that
time, toward the cost of the land for the Pinnacle site.
This was wonderful because it freed the new church
from the normal monthly mortgage payments on the
Presbytery's loan.

Third, Valley would provide "in kind" expenses by
allowing its staff to provide secretarial support, as well
as printing and record keeping. Other clergy staff
assumed many of the responsibilities of my associate
pastor job description, which would be overshadowed as
I focused my time on leadership for the new church.

Valley would highlight its role of "parenting" a new
church by publicly commissioning me, and several of its
members who resided in the new church area, to organ-
ize a new Presbyterian church in north Scottsdale. These
dozen or so families had no idea that they were about to
embark on an exciting growth project, but they all lived
in a two to three mile radius of the new church site.

With this plan in mind, the challenge was to "pitch"
it to presbytery. This model did not fit with the
Presbytery's traditional model for NCD. My plan represented a change.

It was my belief that the Valley-supported model was
very achievable, and I joked about financially-driven
evangelism. I was motivated to make sure that the

new church would be viable enough to cover my compensation as it was being reduced at Valley by one-third each year.

Little did I realize however, how much resentment my model would cause among other recent Presbyterian NCD pastors who had sacrificed their personal income and family life to work in metropolitan neighborhoods at the Presbytery policy of minimum salary plus ten percent. My clergy colleagues felt resentment, envy, and jealousy. I had not anticipated their reactions, but understood their nature. After persuading the appropriate presbytery committees and executive powers, we formed the steering committee in the spring of 1989. Perhaps because the Presbytery was not in a strong financial position to underwrite new church starts in 1989, and continuing through the 90s, they reluctantly agreed to authorize my project with Valley's financial support.

JERRE

There are always tradeoffs with everything in both personal life and business. The tradeoffs Larry engineered were made consciously to create a very different but highly effective startup model. It certainly paid for itself and more, in positive dividends time and again for Pinnacle Presbyterian Church. The organization now has a healthy membership of over twelve hundred, with more than 300 youth participating in church-related activities.

Did Larry navigate around some of the traditional boundaries and conventions of past practice? Yes. Did he improvise, fusing intelligence with faith to succeed where others did not? Yes. Were there conflicts and some very lively conversations? Sure.

However, just look at the result: Larry has created a unique environment capable of producing even more success and growth in the future. That's what a strong leader does—create an environment where people can realize their potential to meet the needs of customers, communities, and constituents—including shareowners, who in this case are those who have invested in the local organization. I would call Larry's approach an example of "people power"—the driving engine of personal engagement that creates sustainable advantage for any organization.

Believe in Angels— Especially When They Believe in You

LARRY

The new model worked! Why? When I first went to the community, I was told that no other church had been able to make it in this community. Up to that time there had been at least three unsuccessful startup churches. The closest to making it was a minister who led a small group of people in a little chapel—which was once part of Greasewood Flats, a local western restaurant. Despite her faith and desire, she wasn't the person to do it.

As a result of this, the folks on our steering committee didn't want to see another lost cause. We realized that we would have to do a lot of marketing and sales to make it succeed. At this time, I went to the members of Valley Presbyterian Church who were living in the area to enlist their support. I got them involved and got them to start speaking to their friends about the church.

Since failure was still not a part of my vocabulary, I was motivated to be successful as a new church development pastor. I wanted the new church to be successful in its ministry to the community and world. Again, as a husband and father, I was financially motivated to provide the best for every member of my family.

What's more, I strongly believed in what I was doing. I truly perceived that the affluent residents of the Pinnacle area needed the good news of the gospel with its message of redemption, reconciliation, and healing— just as much as the low-income citizens in the area. I have always worked on the premise that if I could touch a single business executive or political figure—that they in turn could positively affect the lives of many people working around them. The light must be raised to illuminate and warm the lives of people at every level of accomplishment.

As a twelve-year resident in the Phoenix area, I was familiar with all of the necessary networking resources needed for a new church development. I not only relied on the nearby residents who were Valley Church members, but I knew the value of networking the real estate businesses in the area, the developers, the school systems, and the local homeowners' gatherings. In addition, my years at Valley Presbyterian Church as an associate pastor in Paradise Valley gave me insight and experience ministering with and to highly educated, successful, opinionated, articulate, and generally politically conservative persons. I knew and served with entrepreneurs, CEOs, and venture capitalists—as well as bridge players, lovers of golf and tennis, travelers, and socialites.

I not only had the support of the Valley Church members and friends, but my spouse worked in marketing at the time. Her marketing experience, sense, and expertise enabled us time and again to be perceived as desirable to the area residents.

That's what I think is needed in business—a push-pull leadership. You have to pull people in the right direction—but not tug at them from some far-out point that they won't follow. Similarly, you've got to push people to take the lead. That is something I see time after time in businesses and organizations. So many leaders are not used to doing both, pulling and pushing.

I talked with the steering committee over and over about excellence. We were determined to be fiscally prudent with our resources yet to achieve a level of excellence in the NCD project because we perceived that conspicuous excellence would be essential if we were to attract and win businessmen and families in this neighborhood.

JERRE

When I think of other startups, one of the things that strikes me is the continuous focus on who's paying, and how it all plays out. That goes back to the mission. When I think of new businesses I've helped out over the years that were startups or spin-offs, one of their problems has been that they lost focus on "who's paying." That crimped them significantly when they went to expand.

Once you stop growing, whatever your organization, you've got an entirely different situation; it changes the environment. So the question is always the same: who's paying. Who owns it at the end? Whether it's any startup, profit or nonprofit; it's always the same. At the end of the day, for-profit organizations exist to provide shareowners with great returns.

As we launch and develop startups today there are several ways funding can occur. One is with a group called "angels"—high-level networking individuals who come together to nurture and help by providing funds as well as professional experience. I've seen wonderful examples of that success, and have actually served as an angel, time after time.

A really memorable example was a young man who worked for me at NCR years ago. He was a talented young software developer who was instrumental in creating a tremendously successful database system that was critical in helping us win Wal-Mart's business worldwide.

Some time after Matt Williams left NCR he contacted me saying that he had started a software company in Seattle. His software was designed to provide auctioning capabilities live over the Internet. I gave him a $100,000 investment to help him get started— literally in a garage in Seattle. Matt's software quickly started to gain momentum. He was moving along and progressing nicely when suddenly fortune smiled. That's often what it takes with startups. His software was used on a live auction to sell a major athlete's Heisman Trophy. The next day Matt called me and said, "Jerre, I can't believe this. I have two companies, Yahoo.com and Amazon.com, competing to buy my company. What should I do?"

I said, "Thank the Lord for good fortune, Matt. Make a decision to go to the one you can best participate with in the future." Matt made the decision to sell his company to Amazon.com, and he's still working there as an executive. His shareowners, including me as a funding angel, were rewarded with Amazon shares that we were able to sell on the open market.

That's what is called angel investing. If I think about it, angel investing existed very much with Pinnacle Presbyterian. Valley Presbyterian did wonderful things to ensure success with the startup.

The second kind of sponsors for profit-making organizations are the venture capitalists. (VC.) These are people who provide capital to help start companies with good ideas and, hopefully, help them to become successful. Good venture capitalists are very smart people, astute at understanding ideas and customer needs. Perhaps most importantly, they have the ability to recognize potential in people. Any organization is only as successful as the talent and energy of its people.

I have participated and helped several venture capital companies over the years. A couple of the boards I'm on have outstanding VC members. Their business is very straightforward. They raise money from investors like myself or from institutions. They then hold these funds until they find a creative idea for a startup or a company that needs a second or third round of financing. After investing in a company, they actively participate in board activities and management to make it successful. There have been tremendous success stories over the last few years.

VCs are much more cautious today, after a time when many people have lost sight of real value creation and invested in dot com ideas that would never come to fruition, never be profitable or never have a positive balance sheet. In fact, it's a great concern I have for our country.

We need to get back to what it really takes to create success—with returns that venture capitalists have enjoyed over the years. Hopefully, we'll get back to seeing consistent 20–25% annual returns instead of short-term 80–90% annual returns. The rash of dot com and startup failures that happened in 2000 has stressed many of the VCs to the point that some have gone under. Others today are being very, very cautious. So once again the pendulum swings, and when greed overcomes intelligence, ponderous investment penalties are paid. The pendulum needs to return to the middle—where investment goes to ideas of merit for future dividends.

The wonderful quality of life our country has enjoyed over the past two hundred years is the result of people investing in ideas to help others be successful.

Many of those successes over the years have become great companies today: Microsoft, Oracle, SAP, EBay, Amazon.com, and many more in software and the dot-com world.

The third group is made up of individuals who start their own companies. They scratch along at first, often with very little income. They try to create successes. Many of the small stores you see around the Valley of the Sun are exactly that. An example of a family start-up is Ping Golf Clubs—an endeavor by the Karsten family. Several years ago they used their own ingenuity as capital and barely survived, financially. Today, they are clearly successful.

So in each of these three cases who owns it—and who is paying—becomes a critical question. As Larry writes in this chapter, it's important for a congregation to see the activity and momentum of construction. We've enjoyed seeing a part of the future being shaped before our very eyes—the church and its impressive campus were highlighted with the opening in 2001 of an incredible sanctuary that is both peaceful and stimulating, surrounded by other beautiful buildings. We are very proud of it.

One of the things Larry talks about in this chapter was the decision to be fiscally prudent and yet achieve a level of excellence. Those are great words for any entrepreneur, in fact, for any organization. If we focus on our requirements, if we are fiscally prudent with our resources and yet focus on being the very best at what we do or an outstanding level of excellence, the "who's paying" becomes much clearer. People are eager to help successful people become more successful. The "who owns it" becomes a great story of success for all people involved.

One thing that all good entrepreneurs do, and Larry is a great example of that, is to take informed, intelligent risks aimed at providing future dividends. Bill, Scott, and Lance have also taken risks, and it's proved very successful. Matt's auction software endeavor was thoughtfully developed and marketed with successful results. That model works well. It should be remembered as we move to the next step toward achieving the vision.

PLANNING QUESTIONS

WHO'S PLANNING, WHO'S PERFORMING - AND WHO'S PAYING?

Chapter Three

1. Where will you secure funding for your enterprise? _____

   How will you create an environment where people can realize their potential to meet the needs of the customers, communities, and constituents, including shareowners with an investment in your organization?

   _____
   _____
   _____

2. Who owns your product/service? _____
   Who has a stake in your organization?_____

   _____

   What is their investment? _____

3. How can you be fiscally prudent while maintaining excellence?

   _____
   _____

   How can you focus on your requirements, being fiscally prudent with resources, yet is the very best at what you do?_____

   _____
   _____

   How are you managing your cash flow? _____

   _____
   _____
   _____

4

Putting Values and Relationships to Work

LARRY

Our excitement mounted as the long-awaited moment drew closer—Pinnacle's first worship service, on World Communion Sunday, October 1, 1989. During the previous summer I had met with small groups in private homes in the greater north Scottsdale area. These meetings were mission-critical, but the logistics were sometimes difficult. Barriers were in front of me at every turn.

Chapter 4 discusses the early stages of development and how to:

- Look for creative ways to market.

- Let good values and principles govern you and your business.

- Treat everyone with dignity and respect.

- Evaluate performance and goals in order to become more successful.

And, always remember that strong values and quality relationships create momentum and excitement, which in turn leads to profitable growth for every person involved.

Traditionally, an organizing pastor launches new church initiatives by knocking on residential doors, creating conversations, and inviting people to church. Let me assure you, affluent communities can require a change of tactics. I found that people didn't answer their doors unless they knew who was on the other side. Also, security gate guards don't allow anyone into the community without confirming the visitor's stated destination. Even if a supportive resident invited the pastor into a gated community to go door to door, someone would likely have called the guard to complain. Bingo, out goes the pastor in an embarrassing situation.

To get around this issue, I asked Valley Presbyterian Church members who lived in the neighborhood to host coffees, wine and cheese parties, or desserts. At the first one for Pinnacle, the hosts invited their friends to come hear about the new church. Only one or two showed up. Then, we shifted our approach to invite people over to talk about the neighborhood and the impact of changes and growth in our area. Obvious to me at least, one of the positive changes was a new church.

I started the discussion at these gatherings by asking folks what they perceived to be the really challenging problems in the area. I had someone carefully list their responses on a large note pad, organizing them into reasonable categories. From there, I would move the discussion into how a new church in the area could respond to these problems. Typical problems were population growth, privacy, inadequate schools, churches, and no meeting places. A church was needed not only to meet spiritual needs but also to provide a place where people could come together to form a sense of community.

Many people felt lonely behind all their precautions to remain safe, and saw the new church as a risk-free, secure environment to meet and socialize with others. Even as these residence-based conversational gatherings proved effective, we joked about our "home demonstration" parties.

We turned ourselves into marketing strategists, and we were pretty creative. We sent out bulk mailings to every resident in the zip code areas we had agreed upon with the other Presbyterian Church. In addition to the usual mailers listing time of worship, meeting place, and services offered, we added a newsletter to announce activities and upcoming programs. We also included information about the church, a handy note pad with the church's name and telephone number, and a monogrammed pen on each front door in new housing areas that did not have guard gates. We were on our way.

An obvious form of advertising was to erect a large sign on the church property. But we ran into an unanticipated roadblock from the city. In order to maintain the scenic appeal of Scottsdale, we were not allowed to erect a sign on the property. Nor could we place a sign along the road at a key intersection with directions to the temporary meeting facility. Sign ordinances in the neighborhood are actively enforced by the city. We considered putting one up anyhow, but we knew that when we wanted cooperation and approval from the city on building plans in months to come, we didn't think it wise to make a big issue over the signs. Some boundaries are best left unchallenged.

We were soon to find a way around the sign barrier. We collected lots of old sandwich board signs from a local realtor who used them to announce open houses. We had them repainted with an attractive gold background with navy blue lettering. We discussed these with the city, and were advised that we could place them out on Saturday mornings as long as we retrieved them by Sunday afternoons. It worked! I carried them around in the trunk of my car, drove 50 miles round trip to put them out Saturday mornings, and picked them up on the way home from Sunday worship each week. Eventually I wearied of the chore and paid a local teenager to place and retrieve the signs weekly.

The next concern came from the guard who worked at the gated entrance to the Glenn Moor Clubhouse, our real estate office meeting facility. He had to be assured that he would not be fired for letting cars into the secure community behind the guard-operated gate. Working with his supervisor proved to be an easy task. We arranged to have him leave the gate in the open position on Sundays when the cars would be entering for the church service.

I believed strongly that the more I could get people involved in the actual preparations and activities around the Sunday morning services, the stronger their personal bonds would become in the first few months of this pilgrimage.

Every week, I asked people to help set up and take down the chairs for worship, and scatter hymnals and Bibles on them. This simple act of personal responsibility developed an ownership of our new church project as well as a sense of obligation to be present. It was amazing the help we got from people who typically ask others to set up and take down furnishings in their homes, to clean their homes, and to serve at parties and social gatherings. Yet, each week at worship they gladly helped set up and dismantle the meeting space.

It was as if they needed to be needed, and were glad to assist. Some would even use a vacuum sweeper to clean the carpeting of cookie crumbs dropped from the fellowship coffee hour after church.

In God We Trust: But If You Want to Lead Us, You Better Earn It

It was at this time in world history that the infamous Tienamen Square incident occurred in China. We were all struck by the television image of a single courageous young man standing in personal protest before armed communist tanks as they overran the city of Beijing. To many, this image became a symbol of personal responsibility in the struggle for freedom from oppression. It had an impact on our small group as well, since we felt we were struggling against a number of obstructive influences and people in our quest to launch and nourish a new church.

With all the social, international, political, and economic changes occurring in the world, it was a time when local residents sought security and reassurance in their private lives. Under pressure from the collective voices of freedom, the socialist-imposed wall in Berlin fell, after which East and West Germany were reunited.

Yet in August 1990, the people of Kuwait were attacked, and nightly television news brought images of laser-guided weapons bursting upon the aggressor, Iraq. The economy was sliding. Fear and anxiety arose about the future of freedom. A growing distrust of both business and government dominated local table conversations. After the election of Bill Clinton in 1992, credibility plunged, distrust peaked, and political battles escalated. Suspicions mounted about the funny-money dot coms which were beginning to emerge.

In this dark global context, the radiant light of the gospel message found increasing acceptance in North Scottsdale.

Infused in my soul by my father is one overriding value—to be scrupulously honest in all that I do, which has served me well in my church career. The power of human trust in leadership is an earned trust and delicate alliance; to violate it creates an almost insurmountable sense of betrayal which is nearly impossible to redeem.

It was at this time that a nationally-known televangelist was being sent to prison for fraudulent use of money donated to his cause. Jim Bakker and his wife had built up a television following of Americans who watched as their smiling leader was found guilty of improper use of donated funds. And, at this writing, witness the horrendous widespread betrayal of trust by Roman Catholic priests and bishops in covering up acts of pedophilia in the church in recent years.

Most of us know the difference between a good leader and a good administrator: a leader knows how to do the right things, and an administrator knows how to do things right. Actually, these two observations are not mutually exclusive, but complement each other. Nevertheless, doing the right things has always included an ethical imperative for truthfulness, honesty, and integrity in interactions with people.

JERRE

The issue of trust brings to my mind the values that Larry built into the heart and soul of Pinnacle Presbyterian. I also think of trust as the primary value guiding the companies that I've led over the years. I'll give you some examples of that.

One comes from the early days of my leadership as head coach (CEO) of Legent Corporation, a great software company that was number two in world market share. Its mission was delivering integrated product and service solutions that help customers manage information technology resources. We put a team together from around the world and agreed on which values or principles we would establish as the key criteria for making every business decision. These values would govern the way we would hire and recruit people as well as how we would communicate our values to customers, vendors, shareholders, and communities. Those values follow:

- Actively work together across boundaries to deliver value for our customers, partners, shareowners, and communities.

- Celebrate both individual and team successes. Teamwork is critical.

- Respect the individual and treat everyone as we like to be treated.

- Act in fairness where we respect individual and cultural differences.

- Have integrity where we do the right thing and we are ethical and honest.

- Build trust by keeping our promises and admitting our mistakes.

- Deliver excellence in all that we do and set measures for how we're doing as compared to our competitors—and how well we meet our goals.

- Take accountability and ownership of our individual and team responsibilities and delivering on our commitments.

These are really the Golden Rules for doing business. It's a wonderful set of guiding principles for decision making. We adhered to these principles at Legent Corporation just as we have always set values at other corporations and organizations where I've been fortunate enough to be the head coach, leader or CEO.

Larry set those at the very beginning under the two-pronged goals of excellence and the Golden Rule. He has reinforced his views and practices by emphasizing openness, honesty, quality, and striving to live

in the spirit of Christ—which has found great acceptance and affirmation from the local residents.

I've always said that people are the only sustainable competitive advantage in an organization, and
therefore, we should always treat each other with
equal dignity and respect. If you will, that's a value
that crosses all religious beliefs—even for those who
do not have a faith. It's the only successful way to run
a business.

We the People, In order to Form a More Perfect Union...

LARRY

The concept of honesty and equal treatment was
brought to the forefront of our family experience just
before starting the church. Our adopted, adolescent
daughter was hospitalized at the Menninger Clinic in
Topeka, Kansas. In our experience, everything in the
Menninger medical delivery system was meticulously
honest. Each employee in their system treated our family
members with honesty, respect, compassion, and equality. It made no difference whether we were in a conference in the finance office, admissions office, selecting
food in the cafeteria, or interfacing with the treatment
team and residential care workers in the unit in which
our daughter resided. Every clinic associate treated us

the same—with honor, sensitivity, care, and equality.

I especially remember one family group session in which we met another couple, parents of one of our daughter's peers. We learned that they were a family of national and some international prominence. Yet at Menninger, a local church pastor and his family were being received and treated with the same respect as these influential people! The gratitude we felt for such a reception and equal treatment has never left my memory. I became even more convinced that the same principle needed to be consistently and universally practiced in our church, whether with church officers, Sunday School teachers, people in the pews or the hired help.

The Menninger Clinic experience also underscored the importance of having each component of an integrated system function at an equal level. For the church, all of the complementary pieces of the pie: education, music, fellowship, and pastoral care are equally as important as the prime-time moment of Sunday group worship. If one of the pieces gets less attention and focus, then the whole system is weakened.

One more thing I learned in working with affluent neighbors. Residing in gated communities can create an inflated sense of self-worth and value. Several neighborhood residents lived with private security systems reinforced by guard dogs, as well as a growing distrust of political and economic systems locally, regionally, nationally and globally. Yet our steering committee's emphasis on openness, honesty, equality, and striving to live in the Spirit of Christ was finding great acceptance and affirmation.

JERRE

Larry talks about the importance of every dimension or component of the total church environment. That's true anywhere because the organization is only as effective as the collective efforts of each individual in each position. We can get rid of all of the policy barriers that have been imposed over the years—ones that interfere with the work of business motion—by treating each other with dignity and respect. We can only be totally successful as a company if each of us is personally successful. When we adopt this as a practice, we create a powerful culture where great people are attracted, retained, and perform better.

When I became chairman and CEO of Ingram Micro in the summer of 1996, we were a very successful company enjoying a record year of $8 billion in revenues and almost $100 million of profits. In 1996, we set out with a goal and similar values as those I instilled at Legent. We set out to be the world's largest, most successful provider of services to the entire technology industry. Our goal was to touch every company in the world. With market growth, we believed that we could be a $25–30 billion company in four to five years. Well, in fact we reached over $28 billion in the year 2000, and were listed as the 41st largest company in the United States by Fortune and Forbes 500.

Much more importantly, however, during that time we recruited, hired, and retained thousands of great people. We went from about 7,500 to nearly 20,000 employees during that four-year period. We added dozens of people every week. Orientation included a three-day learning session about our values, customers, and how to strive for excellence. We stressed how every person should be treated with equal dignity and respect. That was critical in our vision and mission "college," if you will, of joining and understanding what our company stood for. It was important in learning and gaining the excitement of being part of such a great company.

I attended those sessions whenever possible, anywhere in the world so I could encourage our new associates. I wanted them to know how important it is to be part of the team and about our exciting future. In the process, I learned from their questions and answers. I found out what was on their minds and what we could and should do better.

I would spend time with similar groups, six to seven months after hire, to ask them to help us to get better by answering three questions:

- What were we doing that we should keep doing?

- What were we doing that we should stop doing?

- What weren't we doing that we should start doing to help every one of us be more successful—and to help our customers be more successful?

Larry points out how key world events unfolded as the church began to grow. During business as well as economic ups and downs, the values Larry instituted in 1989 have stood the test of time. These are the same values I have seen in many businesses and organizations that have operated with integrity.

When we consider our products and services and take them to market, and when we really think about our future, it's critical that we can articulate what we stand for, what our organization sees as its criteria for making decisions, and the kind of relationships it is creating. Because I tell you, in business as in life, the quality of personal relationships is everything. That's the way I do business.

And it is also, if you will, a ray of light from the gospel as Larry and I both see it and believe it. Show me something Christ said and I'll show you a relationship counselor in action whose values are visible to all and who leads by doing.

Strong values and quality relationships create momentum and excitement, which in turn leads to profitable growth for every person involved. I've seen it work in enormous companies as a CEO and seen it work in neighborhood shops as a small boy in Iowa. When I think of profitable growth I think it really is, in essence, driven by learning. Just as my wife and I have been fortunate to learn a great deal during the last six years as members of Pinnacle Presbyterian Church under Larry's leadership, by living what you believe, you can do wonderful things.

Sharing those values and the way of future success enables a startup to become a viable, enduring company. It is truly an exciting time when they start advertising services or products to customers. It's a fun and rewarding time. It's a test of whether we have been on target in our thinking, where we get the answer to many questions. One is: "Are we right?" And, if we are, "How do we gain momentum?" As we discuss the ways an organization can build momentum in Chapter Five, we have felt the energy surging from person to person in our organizations. It is a great time to be part of organizations that are overcoming boundaries and consciously driving and shaping a better future for all members and constituents.

PLANNING QUESTIONS

PUTTING VALUES AND RELATIONSHIPS TO WORK

Chapter Four

1. What creative means of marketing will you use? _____

   _____

   _____

   _____

   Do you have someone on board who can handle the marketing or will you
   utilize an outside consultant? _____

   How much have you budgeted for marketing? _____

   _____

2. How will good values and principles govern you and your business?

   _____

   _____

   _____

3. How will you treat everyone with dignity and respect? _____

   _____

   _____

4. How will you evaluate performance and goals in order to become
   more successful? _____

   _____

5. How will your leadership earn the trust of your customer/clients/constituency
   and as well as your team of employees? _____

   _____

   _____

   _____

6. How will you actively work together across boundaries to deliver value for
   your customers, partners, shareowners, and communities?

   _____

   _____

   _____

7. How/when will you celebrate both individual and team successes?

   _____

   _____

8. Are you able to respect the individual and treat everyone as you like to be treated? _____

   _____

9. Can you act with fairness as you respect individual and cultural differences?

   _____

   _____

10. Do you have integrity to do things ethically and honestly?

    _____

11. Can you honor contracts/promises/covenants thereby building trust?

    _____

12. Will you deliver excellence in all that you do and set measures for how you're doing compared to your competitors? _____

    _____

    _____

13. When you consider your product and service and take it to market, and when you think about the future, can you articulate what you really stand for?

    _____

    What does your organization see as its criteria for making decisions? _____

    _____

    Do you develop relationships that will bring respect and last? _____

    _____

    Will they build momentum? _____

    _____

5

BUILDING RELATIONSHIPS, NETWORKS, AND MOMENTUM

LARRY

The Presbyterian Church, USA (PCUSA) is committed to providing equal opportunities for employment when a local church pastorate becomes available. Thus, when a church is without a pastor, the vacancy is typically advertised nationally for all those interested in applying for the position. On the surface, this seems fair. However, reality is complex, and the Spirit moves "wherever it listeth." A light was shining in North Scottsdale that year, and neither darkness—nor institutional policy—could overcome it.

As you begin your business you begin to gain momentum and grow the business. This chapter discusses how to do this through:

- Building relationships not only with potential buyers, but also with those who can carry your "commercial" to others.

- Understanding the importance of momentum.

- Constantly defining who you are and where you are going as it applies to your vision and goals.

The usual procedure for finding a new 'church development pastor' in Grand Canyon Presbytery was to elect an organizing pastor search committee, advertise the new position nationally, and finally, to select the best candidate. All too often, the new pastor selected was a total stranger to the local community—with no grasp of or line of sight to the many intersecting relationships so critical to the project's success. Although this position was advertised in the appropriate denominational publications, it was generally understood at the presbytery that "the Lord was calling Corbett" to this organizing pastor position.

This rare understanding was something more than spiritual—it was pragmatic. My knowledge of the local network was an advantage and helped to build momentum for support early in the organizing pastor search process. My calling to do so was thus aligned with reality. Once the decision was made, I immediately began to contact a personal network of potential support. The Gospel is firstly relationship-focused, and I was operating in the right mode.

Having worked in the Scottsdale community for seven years at the parent church, my line of sight was broad and intact. I knew how to proceed—but it takes more than one action hero to sound a trumpet, lead the charge and win the oncoming series of battles. I needed what my friend Jerre calls 'people power.' Because of the groundwork our steering committee and I had done, we realized that with the expected population growth in north Scottsdale there would soon be new schools, roads, fire stations, police stations, restaurants, parks, and most importantly, residential developments. In addition, I invested time over many weeks and months visiting numerous residential developments in the north Scottsdale area.

The committee met regularly, and made sure the 'deliverables' materialized: we printed brochures about the new church and I made cold calls on realtors in these developments. The purpose of these calls was to gain the realtors' support, build relationships and gather intelligence. Ordinarily, I would introduce myself, look at their home models on display, engage them in conversation about the size of their project, how the sales were going, and from what part of the country were the new residents moving. I would also tell them that I hoped to help them in their work by providing information about our new church, the first one in a five-mile radius of Pima and Happy Valley Roads. (Actually, it was the first mainline denomination to be present in the community as there was a very small Wisconsin Synod Lutheran Church a couple of miles away.) Conversation centered on our plans for worship, a church school, and parenting classes. I would invite them to visit us in worship to get a grasp of the nature of our congregation. I'd always ask them for permission to leave a few brochures with them. Finally, I made the case that the presence of a mainline church in the neighborhood would help increase residential sales. I made many realtor friends.

Relationship building was a key driver of momentum at Valley Presbyterian Church where I sought to create in-kind support from diverse persons/groups in the congregation. In addition to the financial support, I solicited help from everyone I thought could realistically contribute to our forward motion. I worked with Valley's office staff to print bulletins and brochures, and prepare mailings. I relied on office volunteers to make follow-up telephone calls for the small group meetings we held in homes. I lined up groups of 'Mariners,' adult team members connected to our nationwide church organization, to serve weekly as ushers and greeters as well as parking attendants at the new church worship site. I visited the Director of Music at Valley and persuaded him to "loan" choral ensembles, soloists, and other instrumental musicians to participate in our worship services. I truly believed that the energy and power of music would speak to the souls of worshippers beyond the spoken word. The director willingly accommodated our requests.

The spirit of cooperation in Valley Church was overwhelming. Rarely did anyone respond, at least not to me, that "Gee, isn't it nice that we're starting a new church." Rather, the typical response was "What can we do to help?"—which was delightful to hear. I gladly provided many their next Christian ministry—and put them to work! Clearly, people of all types were getting on board with a supportive network of assistants in moving toward our first worship service.

Momentum was rising. The light was growing stronger. Although the word "momentum" is a concept familiar for both the business community and the church, in ecclesiastical circles one would typically speak of "the leading of God's Spirit." The question can be asked: "When is it momentum and when is it God's spirit?" I would answer that when the Spirit is moving, momentum is present—as well as a kind of synchronicity in the relationships, conversations and events as they unfold in the work of the Kingdom. We felt that God's spirit was present and active. The Steering Committee began each meeting with prayer to seek guidance and God's blessing—and then rolled up our sleeves. We believed that it was essential to "do our homework" by setting strategy, plans, fund raising, and step-by-step follow up. Even though we worked diligently for a successful outcome, we could not manipulate the Spirit of God in the execution of the project. When we recognized God's hand in circumstances, we were simply grateful. That was God's promise, and grace was with us as we executed the vision. Lighting the way: vision, mission, identity and value proposition.

Underlying the growing network of personal support was the crucial performance of the steering committee, and its perception of the new church's emerging identity, vision, and mission. In business, one might call this a 'value proposition'—a promise that sets expectations for 'customers.' I challenged the committee from time to time by asking:

- Who are we?

- Where are we going?

- How will we get there?

- Why would anyone want to join us?

As to "Who are we?" we were not embarrassed about being Christians, literally disciples of Christ. We recognized that to many in contemporary society, the practice of a living Biblical faith seems unnecessary if not archaic. On the contrary, we understood that our faith—and its corollaries—was in fact the guiding light for a shadowy and shallow world. We were confident and connected. We would share that confidence in the weeks and years ahead. And we would find many who wanted exactly what we had.

Through the years I have said to members of Pinnacle Presbyterian Church that I believe that "Jesus Christ is Lord of life." Understand that this is the premise of all we do. However, after that affirmation of faith, articles of theology and issues of doctrine are up for discussion as there have been many changes in the understanding of Christian doctrine through the centuries and recent years. Although we wanted to serve the entire community and in some ways saw ourselves as being a community church, we were in no way reluctant or bashful about practicing our Christian faith, nor our affiliation with the Presbyterian Church, USA.

Connected to the identity question, "Who are we?" were issues of anonymity vs. familiarity. We wanted to create a milieu in the worship space in which a stranger could find a home, yet respect privacy for those not ready to become conspicuous in a public ministry. It was important to create a unique space that would allow persons to reconnect in a relationship with God—without necessarily having to prove they 'qualify' for their reconnection with God. We sought to take all persons and names seriously, but without putting extraordinary pressure on them to sign the charter. (But I surely wanted them to sign the charter!) We have sought to offer a place of worship and spiritual space that is safe—one in which people choose to become acquainted with one another, or remain anonymous. We respect people as individuals to make choices pertaining to their role and place in God's will.

To the second question, "Where are we going?" we focused on a ministry of the obvious—worship, education, music, and service to others in the Spirit of Christ. Our pilgrimage in the development process was not from a stance of coercion to this particular style of religion but from persuasiveness to join us on this pilgrimage of faith.

We strove to create a sense of unity in our forward movement, a unity that was grounded in our faith in Christ as Lord of life. But we sought to make that unity inclusive in a way that recognized the freedom of persons to make choices in their own time frame and of their own free will, and on the road of their personal journey of faith. As Martin Luther wrote three hundred years ago in his essay, *The Freedom of a Christian Man*, we lived with the contrasting stances, that: "In Christ a person is completely free, subject to none. In Christ a person is completely dutiful, servant of all."

Third, some had asked: "How will we get there?" Our meetings and discussions served as a source of continuous planning, learning, strategizing and then doing. And we kept busy—assigning action items and following through. We knew that we would realize the vision by focused execution. It wouldn't happen, as I have said, by wishful thinking.

Finally, we asked ourselves: "Why would folks want to join us?" In the world of business, this is a 'value proposition' and we knew we needed to think about the kind of environment we were creating—and understand that people would perceive value based on the quality of church experience. Although residents in the area were affluent, we knew there was nonetheless a clear spiritual need—a thirst, if you will, driven by loneliness, isolation, and great anxiety about the future. We believed that there was a need for the gospel to be heard, seen in action, and experienced personally. Indeed, we set out to create an environment where that need could be met—in a comprehensive way. We were intentional, inclusive, and focused on this central purpose, enjoying the challenge before us, and growing together in our own faith and discipleship as we journeyed forward together. Sometimes we laughed at our errors, sometimes we cried, and sometimes we were frustrated. But we always were moving ahead.

At this point—and other points along the way, the church itself had needs—and quite often we struggled to regain momentum when it would slip. We needed to move from being groups of people meeting in a clubhouse sales office to a church with its own building, a customized environment that would realize the vision. Inwardly, we needed to move from basic questions about God to a deeper, more mature spiritual life. Paralleling this was the desire for people to accept, and then affirm, the change in their community. We wanted them to make a commitment, get on board, and work toward making the church a reality. We were recruiting action heroes—momentum builders.

One important momentum builder came through a group of hard-working and committed women, led by a member of the steering committee. Even before we had our first worship service, they began to envision having an annual church fund-raiser. They even worked out the details: the event would include tours of three or four spectacular homes in the neighborhood, a bazaar of handmade items by members or friends of the church, and a luncheon served at the local country club. This annual event, known to our community as the *Pinnacle Potpourri*, grew and flourished in support and popularity. It was fun to socialize—and yet it was serious business. As someone observed, "Although our financial needs were great, others in the world had much greater needs than ours," so we annually committed a tithe of our gross income from "Pinnacle Potpourri" to mission projects of the Presbyterian Church in the Synod of the Southwest.

Through the years we have significantly contributed to that mission. And, indeed, it became a model years later when an $8.5 million dollar capital fund drive included a commitment of $100,000 to the local presbytery for new church development in its bounds.

Keep Your Eyes on What You Need to Do Next—and Keep the Momentum

Momentum can shift and change so quickly. When I watch professional football or college games on Saturday afternoons, the television announcer will talk about how the momentum has shifted and changed. First one team, then the other takes the lead. I sometimes wonder how momentum in organization building is different from the momentum being described by television sports commentators?

JERRE

That's a great comparison. I think it's the same, but the time frame is much different. An example is a football game I saw when the home team was leading 14 to zip. They had the ball, two minutes to go in the second quarter, fumbled, and watched the visiting team recover and score. This was a clear momentum change. I could see it. I could almost hear the coach at half time, pumping the home team, saying, "Did you see what just happened?" The home team may be ahead, but after the momentum-shifting interception, they're feeling negative. It's psychological, and it shows in their play. They had all of half-time time to sit and dwell on it. But they also had time to rethink their next move. In business there's a difference: there are no half times, no 'time outs' you can call to stop everything. The game goes on. The motion continues.

You have to act quickly and focus on the next step—execution. You don't have a rest period to think "Gee did I lose momentum or did I gain momentum?"

Another example is Bill Bartzak at MD On-Line. It's taken him about three times as long as he thought it would to revolutionize the industry. The first huge loss of momentum he had was about three years ago, when he realized he would have to get more funding. Talk about loss of momentum. He thought: "I really don't like doing this." It was because he had underestimated the difficulty. Bill's startup would be similar to yours, Larry, in the church. Bill got started, then moved forward with some momentum, and then he ran into a wall. Fortunately in the church initiative we've not hit a wall—but certainly ran a few gauntlets. Momentum has continued. Bill's loss of momentum was not the result of some half-time rest period, but it was because the economic 'wind resistance' put more drag on his momentum than he anticipated.

So, when I think of momentum in business, I think, "Are we meeting or exceeding our expectations in reaching the goal?" It's not "Gee the other team scored" as much as it is "We're going to get where we want to be and we're exceeding our expectations." We focus on owning momentum by focusing on what must happen next—and doing it. It's willpower, yet it's more than that. It's self-discipline, yet more than that. It's a winning expectation—a confidence that refuses to submit to negative impulses. I've walked into so many different companies, offices and spaces over the years. I can tell in ten minutes which side of the momentum they're on. You feel it in the energy—the environment.

LARRY

It's also in the energy of the people. You can sense it around the water coolers, around the offices—and in meetings. It's visible. You see it in the ways people interact with customers and each other. It affects relationships. You read the non-verbals and read between the lines. Momentum, positive or negative, sends out strong vibrations.

JERRE

This reminds me of an article about a company I was leading which appeared in the Wall Street Journal. A reporter was putting together a story on executive compensation. She interviewed me to find out what was going on in the business. My comments to her reflected the positive principles I've always practiced in all the companies I've coached. She acknowledged my remarks as "interesting" but she was skeptical. At lunchtime I had a conference call and offered to find someone to take her to lunch. I heard later that she spent the entire lunchtime asking people if they knew how much their CEO was being paid, trying to spin the issue toward the negative. She had an agenda. To her surprise, they all said things like, "No it's great. He earned it. It's super and we're excited about where we're going." She came back and said the momentum I had going in the company was incredible. She was doing her best to prove a negative. Yet we had momentum—and not even a professional journalist could spin it away.

I say if you've got momentum, great—go, go, go to keep it alive. I think a huge part of the success of this church is that Larry never allowed it to ever lose momentum. Larry has remained focused and active, keeping his eye on the vision and communicating it continuously.

Maintaining Momentum:
The Positive Voice of the Positive Coach

LARRY

It's hard for me to think of how it has happened. I remember a steering committee member saying that she didn't see how we could possibly get this thing done. I always replied in an upbeat positive way. It's part of keeping the vision and using positive thinking. It's almost like being a coach.

JERRE

It is like being a coach. It's also naming and claiming—taking authority and ownership of the situation and making the moment special. When you see a success you name it and claim it. Then, you move on. I see so many organizations that forget to do that. Celebrating even little achievements creates momentum. You do that almost subconsciously. I don't think you can ever do too much of that. In this crazy world we live in today people so much need successes. Even if they're little ones, it's worth recognizing these as acts of positive momentum and so it's great.

LARRY

Plus, it helps everyone's self esteem because they begin to think, "Wow I am part of something that counts." People rise to greatness and success when they feel they are part of a great and successful cause or undertaking. I have seen it.

JERRE

I've said over the years that the CEO is really the head coach. Much of a coach's job is to create and sustain momentum. A good coach does that many ways, and one of the key ways is by focusing every player's attention on what needs to happen next. The coach gets people to look where they are going—because people tend to go where they are looking.

LARRY

Focus may be the most important thing. I think of a coach who at halftime has to keep the team focused and keep momentum. You have to get them believing that they can do again the great things they've done before. A coach needs to continuously remind people of what they've done well—and what talent and skills they have—to encourage and build up. Never let people forget they can win.

JERRE

I believe in communication. Positive reinforcement and positive repetition helps. I repeat what works. The voice of the coach is really critical. A good coach knows he or she becomes the voice inside the head of the players. As a coach and CEO there are four things you've got to do: innovate, motivate, reward, and communicate. You need to focus players in these areas. This is what a coach does. He becomes the positive voice inside their heads—because the negatives can multiply like weeds. So you multiply positives. You have to outnumber them, literally. You have to populate people's minds with positive thoughts—based in reality and what they know they have done before and can do in the hours, days and years ahead. And in this church, Larry, I know has done that over and over again for the last 15 years.

Momentum Is More Than a Feeling: the Whole World Is Watching— and Talking

LARRY

The other question is, "How do people read signs of momentum in business and the church?" It's like Jerre said. You can walk into a meeting and perceive which way the momentum is moving. What do people perceive as the signs of momentum?

JERRE

In business, it's growth first. Are you hiring people? Are you growing the organization? The same goes for the church. People want to be part of a group of successful Christians in a growing, life-affirming environment. It's a powerful force of attraction. In business we want to join a proven winner.

Another sign of momentum is in the nature of the people who populate the environment. Before they join, people ask: who else is part of this team? Is there someone whom I really respect on the team? Every company has its legends—its larger-than-life action heroes—ordinary people who do the extraordinary. If the star performers are there, that creates a lot of momentum.

Third, who is talking about my business? Are we receiving positive coverage in *Business Week* or The

Wall Street Journal? I was thinking about what Larry said after the Presbytery meeting a month ago. We clearly made a statement about whom we are. Now, they are undoubtedly talking about it. When the press finds you interesting and wants to write about what you are doing, you know you have a compelling story. Momentum is very important. People are always looking to see if it is a blip or if it's sustained. That's the sign most people look for. In business you use numbers for it. How much are your revenues? How has your net income grown? What was in your quarterly report?

Synchronicities Tend to Multiply: Momentum Leaps When Every Referee Call Goes Your Way

LARRY

In a football or basketball game, when the momentum shifts and when a team begins to pull away, they clearly have the momentum, the movement and the energy going with them. It seems as if they get the referee's calls going their way, too. You just see it happen. It's like it's a subconscious thing on the part of the officials. Does that happen in business and who makes those calls?

JERRE

Sure it happens in business. The referees are analysts, investment bankers and to some degree the media. It starts when you get calls from them. Customers see it and it adds to the momentum. Of course, customers make calls too. Customers can always tell you and others how you're doing—especially the shrewd ones. I'll never forget the 2002 Michigan-Iowa game. Michigan had the momentum after they scored just before the end of the first half. By half time Iowa had ten and Michigan had six because they missed the extra point. Michigan starts the second half by marching down the field and they scored so it's 9 to 10. Michigan intercepts a pass. You think, this is it—that was the "big play". However, then, Michigan fumbled on the next pass and Iowa picked up the momentum and that really was the game. I'll never forget that. It was momentum, shifting momentum. Iowa won 30 to 9.

LARRY

I'm wondering if that occurs in the church with a local congregation that has a program going and gained visibility in the community?

JERRE

Our Sunday school and preschool have that kind of public visibility and momentum. People know it, they feel it, and they are proud of it.

LARRY

One of our members recently called to set up an appointment with me. He was dragging his feet in enrolling his three-year-old in preschool. He debated the merits of keeping the child protected at home for another year versus putting him out into a risky world. He related to me that he had been in a business meeting with a coworker and his client. Somehow the subject of this preschool came up. The client related his wife had gotten in line at five in the morning in order to make sure their child got registered in our preschool. Imagine that! The client was emphatically raving about what a great preschool we had. The man had no clue Marty was a member of our church. Now he has his child enrolled. Talk about synchronicity! These are the kinds of inexplicable synchronicities we see when we have positive momentum.

JERRE

We were recently at a party where I was sitting next to a woman from Germany. The subject of the church came up and she remarked, "Oh, that's the one that is growing so rapidly. We'll have to try it sometime." Word travels. Another time I saw momentum grow for the church was when we moved into the new sanctuary. Although some of the earliest members had a tough time being pulled from the intimate chapel into the large sanctuary, in general people really are excited about the sanctuary. There's new life, a new environment, and new momentum.

Three Ways of Looking at Momentum: the Principles in Business Experience

---

JERRE

In the mid to late '90s, when the incredible stock market boom was going on and people were willing to invest in almost anything that had a dot com at the end, it was difficult to attract and retain great people. I think of Lance and Cory in Orange County, California, doing their best to bring in really good talent to help them bring an exciting new business to reality. Earlier in Lance's career he spent a couple of years as an executive search firm recruiter and was a very successful one. Lance was able to draw on his past talents and experience to lure a tremendous CIO from Phoenix to Orange County. The allure was he would have an opportunity to build from scratch a truly new, exciting computer-driven system using all the new tools and technology available at the time. He brought people with him.

I think of Bill Bartzak out on the East Coast, and his MD On-Line. Bill was constantly battling to attract good people. For startups, building momentum begins with finding the right people. Then, as we talked earlier, persuading people to invest. And, then, take the huge step of moving that first product to market. In each of the cases of the three companies I've talked about, that first step is truly momentous. It's one that people remember forever.

For sure, I can think of comments each of the entrepreneurs has related, describing selling that first customer. In Bill's case it was a large insurance company. He went to them hat in hand with his software and said, "I can go to doctor's offices via CDs. I don't even need to be there. They can install my product in five or ten minutes. No matter where they are or live, using the Internet or even a more traditional method, our system will work and provide paperless documentation—effortlessly." Needless to say, that was revolutionary, and it was also a little hard to believe. So he had to show it working. Bill had a huge challenge to build momentum. He made a very smart move and that was offering this particular insurance company the opportunity to test his product with one hundred customers—doctor's offices. The customer chose to see how it would work. Bill followed up with his very small team and in each case called the doctor's offices to make sure they knew how do to a very simple installation. They were off to the races.

Momentum comes very quickly and carries people along. In this case, it came by word with Bill. Bill was busy flying around the country giving speeches, appearing on national TV, and explaining what his company and his products could do to streamline and improve efficiency for the tremendously expensive medical industry in the United States.

About the same time, Lance and Cory were wrestling with the challenge of a very long sales cycle of convincing large corporations that their systems, the Isernhagen solutions, could save them millions and millions of dollars each year. They used a success story from a couple of Goodyear plants where Isernhagen had dramatically improved the safety record as their "proof of the pudding," so to speak. I can remember their frustrations and how slow the startup was, with very little momentum going on because they had to work their way up through large corporations, many of them quite bureaucratic.

Part of their challenge was that companies see and deal with the work-injury problem in pieces: medical, replacement labor, training, risk management, insurance, and legal issues. It was difficult to find a decision-maker or effective internal champion. Leading hospitals and medical centers in the United States recognized the Isernhagen system as the "Gold Standard" and Germany and Switzerland had adopted it as a national standard. However, major employers had yet to understand and appreciate the value of a service that could save them millions of dollars. Although it took much longer than anticipated, WorkWell succeeded in selling to a few large employers. Sales momentum was created when they demonstrated a consistent trade record of significant savings for the early adopters. That momentum continues to build today.

In each case I think there are a couple of keys. One that we've talked about before is sticking to your focus and making sure you're recruiting the very best people that embrace your values.

Second, is being very attentive and listening very carefully to the customer, recognizing how your systems need to change to meet their needs and then moving forward.

The last example is of Scott at GolfLogix. He started out with a system that was sold exclusively to private and public golf courses through distributors in the United States. Scott and his COO flew to Europe in the spring of 2002 on a shoestring, at the back of the bus. He arrived in Spain early in the morning and spent the day mapping out, via satellite communication, a golf course for potential distributors. The next day those distributors signed an exclusive agreement with GolfLogix, including a significant up-front investment. They recognized what great potential was being offered. Of course, they had to make modifications to account for the metric system. The momentum is now building very quickly in Europe. By the summer of 2002, they were in the process of identifying possible appropriate partners in Asia, starting in Japan and Korea. My guess is that they will soon have tremendous momentum there as well.

They, too, saw the importance of listening to potential customers carefully and being flexible. They found a parallel demand to provide a hand-held unit that wasn't rented or used on carts by golf course managers but, in fact, can be sold at retail in sporting goods stores throughout the United States. For five or six dollars a month you can get, through the Internet, all of your golf scores and yardage hits documented in order to learn what you're doing. You can improve ability with great data and "facts as our friends," as I often say, through the use of the GolfLogix retail system that will be introduced in the future.

So in each case, building momentum took a very different direction, a different start, staying flexible, listening externally to customers, recruiting great people and maintaining focus on what needs to happen next. Just as Larry talked about accepting change, affirming change, and supporting change, wonderful words for building momentum, the same is true in every organization I've seen that's been successful in the second half of the 1990s and early 2000s.

On the other hand, we've all seen a lot of companies who have failed in the last few years. They started with an idea—or solution—a value proposition, but they weren't built on creating real shareowner value. They didn't gain momentum and keep it going by being very focused on customers. Many of them first hired a public relations person and a financial person who could talk to the analysts when they went public. Clearly there the idea was to create short-term wealth for the original investors and members of the company—but not a sustainable competitive advantage that yields dividends over time. We are still paying the penalty of that incredible dot com bubble.

Alan Greenspan pointed out in 1998 that people were investing in ideas that would never be profitable, with firms that did not have good balance sheets. Nonetheless, we can learn from those that failed and those that have become successful. In each case, the successes were based on building momentum, recruiting and retaining great people, staying externally focused, committing to a true foundation of values, and helping others be successful. The failures were very short-term focused attempts to create wealth for a few.

Building momentum is really one of the fun parts of developing and coaching any organization. Having been able to witness and be part of the momentous growth and success of Pinnacle Presbyterian Church for the last six years has been one of the highlights of my wife's and my life in church. We have belonged to 15 different churches in our moves all over the world. There's not a church we've ever seen that we're more proud of or that we're happier to participate in than Pinnacle Presbyterian. That's because there are wonderful people with Larry leading, a great staff, with people throughout the church coming from all walks of life. They want to share ideas and be a common Christian community in reaching out to help others. That momentum continues and will continue.

There's always a critical point, a pinnacle point, in every organization. In the case of Pinnacle Presbyterian Church it was the opening day. In the case of most companies, it's their founding day, when they receive funding and actually hand out or mail certificates of share-ownership to their investors and give options to their original associates or employees. In both cases it is a very memorable day that really sets the stage for the future. That's what we will cover in Chapter Six.

PLANNING QUESTIONS

BUILDING RELATIONSHIPS, NETWORKS, AND MOMENTUM
Chapter Five

1. Where will you build relationships with potential customers and with those who can carry your "commercial" to others? _____

   _____

   _____

   _____

2. How will you build and sustain momentum? _____

   _____

   _____

   When you reach plateaus, and/or lose momentum, what will you do to restart it? _____

   _____

3. As you kick off and grow how will you constantly redefine who you are and where you are going in relationship to your vision? _____

   _____

   How will you sell your vision to new investors? _____

   _____

   _____

4. Will you be prepared to act quickly and focus on the next step?_____

   _____

   _____

   Will you be prepared to make decisions without the luxury of thinking, "Gee, did I lose momentum or did I gain momentum?" _____

   _____

   _____

5. Momentum is related to answering "Are you meeting or exceeding your expectations in reaching the goal?" _____

   _____

6. Do you like being a coach/cheerleader/referee and trainer all at the same time? _____
   Which do you really prefer? _____
   Which do you excel at? _____

7. Focus is a critical ingredient. How will you sustain it? _____
   _____
   _____

8. Who is talking about your business? _____
   Are you receiving positive encouragement from your customers and the environment? _____
   _____

9. What is the role of communication and advertising? _____
   _____

10. Momentum comes very quickly and carries people along, often by word of mouth. Can you structure that form of communication? _____
    Why? _____
    Why not? _____

11. What provision(s) do you have to stick to your values, remain focused, and recruit the very best people? _____
    _____
    _____

12. How will you be attentive and listen carefully to the customer, recognizing how your systems need to change to meet their needs and then move forward? _____
    _____
    _____

6

GREAT ANTICIPATION: NOW THAT WE'VE BUILT IT, WILL THEY COME?

LARRY

As the momentous hour approached—opening day for the new church—a sense of nervous expectancy was rising. We felt we were bringing a child into the world. And in a way, it was true. We were creating a new environment, a new experience—and a new community. With anxiety and deeply hopeful anticipation, we wondered:

- Would people come?
- Who would come?
- How many might come?
- How would they respond?
- Would they sense the presence of God?

- Would this experience meet a spiritual need?

- Would they come back the following Sunday?

The steering committee had spent time and energy to establish two clear objectives for the opening day worship experience. First, was to communicate the image, look and feel for the church we were striving to create. We knew how important the first impression would be for those who showed up. We wanted this to set the course for the next twenty years, an image which demographic projections indicated would support a large suburban, neighborhood church of fifteen hundred to two thousand members.

Our new worship experience would include:

- Traditional Geneva robe for the minister.

- Distinguished music provided by a choir, small ensemble or soloist.

- Informative, easy-to-follow bulletins with a printed order of worship that encouraged participation while providing theological structure.

- Responsible child care for infants and toddlers, and a church school for children, preschool through high school, during the worship service.

Moreover, we believed that the total quality of worship experience must be distinctive. Excellence would be our aim—to bring glory to God and to speak to the spiritual needs of the people who would worship with us.

Through excellence and conspicuously high quality, the north Scottsdale community would hopefully make a commitment to join this pioneering adventure, and a new Presbyterian Church would become a flourishing reality.

In Chapter Six we emphasize:

- Everything must be done with excellent quality and service.

- You must look ahead to the ideal and work backwards to see what has to happen to make it a reality.

- It is very important to understand how a decision in one area may affect other areas; think systematically.

JERRE

The ability to work backwards from the future by establishing a clear vision is critical. When we create an environment that affects so many lives and livelihoods, we need to look ahead 10, 15, or perhaps 20 years and realize what we really want to be and what we want the organization to look like and make possible. Then, we communicate that, over and over. This is step number one in an environment where great things can happen. However, if we merely 'ad lib' our way forward, incrementally, that is, making it up as we go, we may never realize our potential—or ever fulfill a higher goal. We'll make progress and we'll certainly be proud of the progress we've made, but it will never be the tremendous explosion of people power available to every organization.

To get the power of vision working for an organization, a leader needs to articulate, and re-communicate the success story that we will become—before it happens. You have to set and communicate goals and identify targets if you expect to create a serious need-meeting environment. Sir Edmund Hillary did not reach the summit of Mt. Everest just by walking around.

Larry and his committee established a vision, set goals and then created an environment in which a church could grow—for the next 20 years. You can see how it allowed the church to work that future backwards into a "present defining moment." Vision enabled them to make the tremendous strides of success starting with very few people. It is now well on track to become a church of 1,500 to 2,000 members—which was articulated early on as the vision back in 1989.

The second thing Larry talks about is the importance of excellence as a key ingredient of everything the church undertakes. At the very beginning he set the stage of focusing on a true and critical value—being the very best possible. This is important because people are compelled to support quality. They are attracted and engaged by excellence. And when your mission is to change lives and elevate people, this becomes ever more essential.

The Process Begins:
One Busy Day at a Time

LARRY

When the first Sunday of October 1989, arrived, the Steering Committee and I made an early-morning start to move office desks, turn off telephones, and set up chairs for the first worship service. This was office space—and it was about to become holy ground. Yes, the first 'conversion' was the room itself!

A piano had been donated by a local family and was in place. The pianist arrived with the soloist to practice before the service began. To the sound of their impromptu rehearsal, tables were set up with refreshments on the shaded patio that surrounded the office facility. We put borrowed hymnbooks and Bibles on each white folding chair. Ushers with nametags were ready with plenty of bulletins. Parking attendants were on hand. Flowers had been delivered for the communion table (in actuality a table where agents sat with potential home buyers six days a week seeking to close a deal) in the front of the newly-purposed worship space.

Suddenly, it was time for the first pilgrims to arrive. Cars started to cruise through the guard gate, and were given a friendly greeting by the gate-guard (I had suggested to him what to say) who advised folk to "proceed to the Glenn Moor Clubhouse, that is, the present and future Pinnacle Presbyterian Church."

As it came time for worship to begin, over thirty residents from the target area were in place for this worship service. This number, coupled with nearly thirty

Valley Presbyterian Church volunteers, created a feeling in the limited space that there was a good crowd of folks for the first worship service.

Because it was World Communion Sunday, I delivered a message that day which addressed the different forms that the church takes in its ministry. This ranged from large cathedrals to inner city storefront churches to chapels on military bases and in hospitals, to suburban churches to rural white-clapboard churches in small villages to house-churches and temporary worship areas throughout the world. I talked about the image of the church as a tree of life, and our little congregation was a new leaf, not even a twig. Yet this new church community would shoot forth, grow and mature as part of the universal tree of life, the Christian church, rooted in Christ, to serve specifically the north Scottsdale community. Its outreach, together with the universal church, would serve as one of many thousand points of light around the globe.

The opening-day music seemed to peal from the highest elevations of heaven, creating a feeling of celebration and joy beginning with *Joyful, Joyful We Adore Thee* and continuing as the soloist sensed and shared the uplifting spirit. Although the total number of people in the space was not a large number by most church attendance standards, the singing in the small room resounded with joy and enthusiasm.

The handful of children who were in attendance went with three Church School teachers (a mother and her two teenage children, both of whom would soon attend Harvard University) and headed to the tennis courts for the outdoor Church School.

At the conclusion of the service cookies and iced tea and coffee (traditional Presbyterian goodies) were enjoyed by all. As the cars began to pull away and disappear back into the greater neighborhood, the steering committee and I sat down to assess how it went. What did everyone think? In short, it went well. We were all very pleased and excited. Moreover we were eager to see a similar positive response the following week.

Yes! We were on our way! The birth of a church, with all the dreams and visions of the future so similar to the birth of a child to a family who have high hopes and dreams for a new child and its promising future. However, being goal-oriented by nature, we immediately began the next step of following up on plans for the second, third, fourth service, etc.

A new child takes a lot of nurturing, feeding, holding, rocking, and sleeping before being able to crawl and move to maturity. We had much work and energy to spend just to get to the crawling stage. One challenge I had was managing my professional image as an organizing pastor who is going solo and doing everything— along with being a distinguished pastor who would be head of a 1,500–2,000 member church.

JERRE

Larry had to be jack-of-all trades from the start and get all of the processes in place from the very beginning, gradually building a much larger organization. I think that's part of the reason we've gone from zero to where we are so smoothly compared to others.

Larry put himself right in the center and took personal ownership of the experience. I'm sure that took a lot of energy and commitment. He knew he was creating something new—taking an unconventional approach. Larry looked at what needed to happen tomorrow as well as keeping an eye on what was happening at the moment.

The Work of Execution: Building a Great Dream Means Building a Great Team

LARRY

Jerre, have you known anyone in business who has done that, and has used that kind of a model? You've talked about AOL. Was Steve Case an example?

JERRE

He's a pretty good one, actually. Plus, it's about the same time frame. Most people probably would have smiled at you in 1989 when you said we were going to have 1,500 to 2,000 members. In the same way most people sure didn't believe Steve. They thought he was goofy—that his dream would never happen.

One of the interesting aspects is the way you

brought in people to help with leadership. Steve did that too. There's one thing that he's probably not as happy about now as he would have been. He sensed the need to bring in an incredibly talented group of people, just as you have here. He also cleaned out the ineffective ones, just as you did. The mistake he made was he brought in a COO and let him run everything day to day. That didn't work. I think it lasted two months before he changed it. If he would have brought in someone like Duane Holloran, as you did, and worked as a team I think it would have been better for Steve.

LARRY

Duane realized that the buck stopped at my desk. More than that, he knew we weren't looking for a "yes" person as associate pastor but one who was in step with the very clear goals and vision toward which the church was moving. Duane and I talked about that. I told him I would give him freedom to develop his ministry here. Wilson Kilgore, at Valley Presbyterian Church, did that for me. I always appreciated this freedom. I told Duane that I did have one condition I insisted upon: I did not want to be blind-sided, just as I would try not to blind-side him.

The important thing was to work toward the goals of this church and be a team. That simple understanding between us I believe allowed him to blossom.

JERRE

And it took a huge load off of you. I've thought about that as we've worked through this book. You've evolved it into a thriving community, not just the job you do today, versus what you did 12–13 years ago. It's an evolution of an entire community. Certainly, your sense of having a guy like Duane here was important.

In the same way, Steve knew he needed help but he approached it in a conventional sense: "Okay, I'll go play CEO or whatever that is and I'll bring this guy in to do all the day-to-day stuff." That works sometimes, but often it doesn't.

You need to evolve the entire organization. I think about the tough decisions you had to make. When you removed people from the organization, it was because they had become barriers to success in the church. Sometimes even barriers to their own success. That needs to be a quick history lesson on how you started this organization and then carried it forward. It was like you had a natural instinct for creating an organization. Some pick up this knowledge in books but it goes beyond what's in books—it's what's in the leader.

LARRY

I know what you mean and yet—it is, and it isn't instinctive. The doctor of ministry program I was enrolled in at McCormick Seminary was most helpful because they taught me to think systematically and see the whole church. Typically ministers do not think about it, and they don't realize that a Sunday school church teacher who does something off-the-wall impacts the whole church. They don't get it.

The second thing I learned in that program was I could not run around putting fires out. It was setting goals and then controlling the process that worked. I had to allow the board to work with me and set the goals. I have no control over what these people are going to say or do, but I can control the process. When you work through problems controlling the process, everyone can go away feeling satisfied. People also feel relief because a process is in place to deal with the situation.

JERRE

In my reading and career I've seen many examples of what worked and what didn't work. When I first was invited to join a corporate board of directors I was really young, in 1975 or '76, and I almost said no. Then I realized I would learn from the examples around me. Looking back, I see I had to learn from book knowledge, and from example—while my professional instincts developed from the conditioning of those who were fulfilling roles and building futures around me.

LARRY

I also learned by example. For instance, I think of the first church I served in Cleveland, where the minister had come there in the mid to late '60s. He called me to be his assistant. His predecessor had the session meet

once a year at the Union Club for cocktails. The rest of
the year they let him run the church. In the sixties, institutions didn't tolerate that any more. They began to
want a voice. Subsequently, he resigned.

The man who took his place wanted management by
objectives and participatory management. He wanted to
get people involved, but he didn't know how to do it.
So, he relied on executives and lawyers in the church
who did know how to do it. In this way I learned from a
GE executive in incandescent lighting, Al Makulec. It
was before computers, and he had a mind that could
bring together relevant information from R&D, marketing, production and sales. He would then make decisions on which products GE would invest in, produce,
and when as well as how many. I began to learn to think
systematically from him. He chaired a transition committee that included professors from Case Western
Reserve, big law firms, and business to set goals and
help the church make the transition from one run by
one person to a working board.

JERRE

We're now hitting two subjects. One is how you build
processes all the way. The second, equally important
is 'how I learned to do it.'

LARRY

I think we learn this ability in three ways: by doing,
studying, and observing people. We learn from people

who see potential in us and ask us to be on the boards. They became mentors for both of us.

JERRE

If you can, you need to go find someone like that. Mentors are valuable. It would have been easier if someone had shared some insight in the beginning. At the end of the day, when you've had a problem and you've narrowed it down to a decision group, you want as small of a group as you can get or you're not going to solve it. Yet, you want to do it so everyone still feels present at the table. It's important for everyone.

LARRY

I like your observation that people want to feel a part of it. I really believe problems are not solved by boards sitting around the table, hand wringing, saying, "What are we going to do?" Boards function best when a task force or committee brings a list of alternatives to them. They still need time to perceive the problem and wrestle with it and not assume that all is well.

JERRE

When everything is in great shape, it can be easy. However, when you have an issue, it's harder to get through the work and get it to play out appropriately.

Yet we need to get every moose on the table. What I mean by that is to get the unsightly issues out in the open for free, air-clearing discussion. Shine the light of leadership openly on every obstructing issue. A leader must communicate, and encourage communication. Enlightenment means bringing to light what is not working—and turning negatives into positives. Radiate light in every corner. Examine everything—and then act quickly and decisively to take the next step in delivering the vision. However, also be sure to spotlight what's going well! Leaders need to call attention to the many things that are indeed working! Celebrate the good things. Identify every way we are doing well—and acknowledge those who are doing so. To focus the light on what we are doing well in any organization means celebrating our accomplishments.

Celebrate on Purpose:
Light Up the Environment

LARRY

Our opening day experience was so encouraging— almost electrifying in its excitement. Yet it was a rare moment. How does an organization like ours replicate that? Or is it even possible? Can we re-create that 'opening day experience' time after time after time for new members? How do we do that?

JERRE

As I said, I have found it to be effective and energizing to create an environment where we celebrate every success, however large or small. Recognize, people, milestones, wins, steps forward. Commemorate how far you've come. In organizations I've led, we made it a point to celebrate events and take time to step back and appreciate our progress, and then go forward. We truly need to celebrate more frequently. I admit it can be much harder to differentiate 'special' events in the church, because the very nature of worship experience is itself celebration. Yet the essence of positive reinforcement is in publicizing and perpetuating progress.

LARRY

Some events we celebrate are not local—rather they are imposed upon us because of the official institutional calendar. Many Sundays are predetermined days of recognition on an international scale—with a theme, agenda or call to action: Missionary Sunday, World Hunger Sunday, and the like.

JERRE

Most of us as leaders and people of faith are aware of the global picture. And we are always challenged to manage and balance the macro and the micro-directing energy, expectations, and priorities. Yet I can tell you that keeping things simple is the best approach. For instance, we always celebrated November 1 at Ingram Micro because that's the day we took the company public. We had a big breakfast for all of the executives around the world. We did a ten-minute video taking them back to the founders in California. It was so powerful. We always made sure that we celebrated who we were, where we were, and here's where we're going. You can do that in an hour and shut down everything around the world. It's so powerful.

I think congregations need this. It's so important for the church to celebrate and restate the vision as we get bigger. It helps people connect. By far the most successful celebration I was ever part of was the 100th anniversary of Honeywell. We had an incredible head of public relations. She decided that for all the big trade shows we would dress as we did 100 years ago and talk about how Honeywell got started 100 years before. We also hired some professional actors and actresses. Those booths were standing room only. It was just marvelous to watch. I was dressed in period clothing, also. Then, at the end of the evening we had singing, dancing, and laser light shows.

We had a 20% increase in the top line that year. I swear—it was because of the energy from this event. I always worked hard with all the organization to find ways to name it, claim it, and celebrate it. This is a wonderful story that people who weren't here before need to know and feel a part of today.

LARRY

One of the things we did at Valley every three or so years was have a special dinner for all the elders and deacons and their spouses, and we did some of the same things. We would focus on how far we had come, who helped us make progress, and look to our future aspirations. We need to do more of that. We also need to do this with our north Scottsdale winter residents. I think we're missing the boat in January and February. We need to have a brunch for all the winter visitors. They would appreciate it, I think. And they've shown it: at Valley Presbyterian winter visitors donated a great, state of the art $15,000 sound system.

JERRE

I think social organizations like the church need to insert these kinds of things because it's uplifting for them. Isn't there a passage in the New Testament that reads: "Let all things be done for edification?" I'm sure of it. The purpose of gathering together is to elevate, inspire, build up and motivate people—to renew them and help them share the joy of their best experiences with others. Not only in church, but also in business, because people need to integrate their personal and business lives. People need to be who they are and celebrate the good things.

LARRY

It helps people affirm the identity of the organization and become an important personal part of it. They need to know they are connected to a greater cause—a transcending purpose and vision that calls each one of us to contribute to creating a higher quality of life for those around us.

JERRE

Right, and in that way the Christmases and Easters become even more meaningful. Those events are much bigger than the church, clearly, and people need to connect and comprehend the tremendous scope of all they represent. People need to see that they are renewing their own lives in the greater context of the ongoing, life-affirming, Christ-affirming movement we are engaged in. It stretches the imagination, sharpens the awareness, deepens relationships, encourages self-realization, and it helps stimulate a grand sense of what we are about.

Breakthroughs Can Be Achieved— With the Explosive Power of Personal Commitment

LARRY

As the church moved through its formative life of the next months and years there were challenges related to slow growth and unanticipated plateaus we encountered. In order to be chartered by presbytery the project had to meet a membership requirement of 100 persons. When we reached 70 it seemed that we had settled on a plateau that was hard to climb away from. Nothing we seemed to do would move us upward and into higher achievement and growth. It did not feel good to be stuck on 70 charter members when we needed 100.

Although the Steering Committee and I were clearly working to achieve a goal of 100 persons in order to be chartered by the Presbytery as a particular church, privately, I was still under consideration to be called as a pastor of a tall steeple church elsewhere in the land. The risk of personal failure in this new church project continued to gnaw at my self-confidence and thus I continued to interview for other potential pastorate positions even though working diligently on the new church project. I continued to be rejected by search committees.

Coming in second place is not fun in spite of the old Avis rental car ads that say 'we try harder.' Rejection hurts. It angers and saddens. It can either cause one to give up and quit or be motivated to pursue other options. I couldn't discern the cause of the rejection.

Was I being rejected because I was an associate pastor and not preaching weekly, or because we had black/white biracial children, or because one of our children was a victim of chronic mental illness? I also wondered: was I just not good enough?

Finally, my wife, Meredyth, and I sat down and had a serious conversation. Were we going to make an ultimate commitment to this new church project or continue to put ourselves through the arduous clergy relocation search process and seek a call elsewhere? After much anguish, prayer and reflection we decided to put our house on the market and make public our commitment to this new church development (NCD) project. It became apparent to us that it is very difficult to do community development when we lived 25 miles away. It also meant taking my dossier off the market and ending my search for another position.

That Sunday I announced to the NCD congregation that we had put our house on the market which meant we were going to buy a house near the new church site. To my absolute surprise the congregation responded with enthusiastic applause! I was unprepared and stunned at their reaction, and immediately realized the extent to which people in new church projects are committed to the leader. There are typically very few programs in NCD work, no permanent buildings, very limited staff, usually only volunteer staff, and in our project, almost everything revolved around my leadership and the very supportive work of the steering committee. It was then I realized that the 70 persons who had already signed the charter were pleased to know that I had also made a commitment to continue with this work and not leave for greener pastures somewhere else.

I also realized that I had been expecting them to make a commitment when I had not previously been willing to share that commitment myself. Not a good moral position to be in, much less one of leadership. It was a matter of a few weeks before these seventy persons suddenly found others to invite to become part of Pinnacle Presbyterian Church. And, in November 1991, we were chartered with 109 members.

Nevertheless, the plateaus continued to haunt us. They manifest themselves in the form of limited financial resources, need for volunteers to serve in critical positions such as church-school teachers, and the like. We are always looking for the next breakthrough. When you have no more homes to mortgage, what do you do next? Breakthroughs can also be triggered by fresh blood— new people on the scene who can generate fresh energy and momentum.

One of the most powerful energizers to Pinnacle church—who helped lift us up from a series of plateaus—was a student intern pastor, Janet Arbesman, in 1994. She was a powerhouse of inspiration. She joined us at a critical time—when we moved into the new chapel and classrooms. Janet eagerly accepted her role as the first Director of the Preschool and helped to get it opened in September 1995. The school opened with 16 three- and four-year-old students and two teachers, plus a board of directors who did the necessary preliminary work of getting the school incorporated and a 501 c 3 nonprofit tax status. Momentum and flexibility became the two key factors in our giant step into the future.

JERRE

In business much the same thing happens when opening day has come and gone, or when a startup opens its doors—for its second day, or month, or year. Businesses seek breakthroughs. Again, you reach out to the future vision and work backward to determine what needs to happen next. I think of Steve Case, who more than 15 years ago, was sitting with little money. He was trying to think of how to start up an organization that later became known as America Online (AOL.com). He hit plateaus and he made breakthroughs. Today his vision is a reality with over 35 million members paying monthly or hourly subscriptions and dues to use an incredible technology vehicle. It's based on the idea that we can sit in a room in our house and touch the world on every subject in any way that we so choose. When Steve was starting, he had a clear vision that someday every country in the world would be using an Internet system. That someday every household and every business would have at its fingertips the tools that we have today. He, starting up with his company, could create a very user-friendly environment. Again, Steve was very focused on a level of excellence in responsiveness, and providing the things people wanted most. He listened to customers. It is incredible to believe how young AOL truly is.

It is interesting today when I read negative articles (and I read far too many trivial downside pieces in the media today) about AOL. People forget what an incredible thing has been created, what an incredible organization. It is still evolving forward around the world today. He has never lost the excitement of the vision he has created. He has shown a strong leadership in reaching out to the future and setting the vision and working backwards from it—that creates a momentum we can replicate each step of the way.

To master the excitement and positive energy of the 'opening day' experience, we need to communicate, celebrate and replicate the compelling power of our vision and mission, time after time. For example at Pinnacle Presbyterian, we have one-hour new member meetings on the last Sunday of each month. We bring in prospective members to learn about the history of Pinnacle Presbyterian. They share their ideas and have their questions answered about Presbyterians. Perhaps, most importantly, they become "connected" to a group of wonderful people who want to openly embrace and bring in newcomers. That shows the progress that has come from that very critical opening day and reaching out to the future.

When I think of some of the entrepreneurs I've worked with, I've seen them thrive in a very short time because they set that vision for the future and worked backwards. They articulated the dream and put the real processes in place on that opening day— and replicated that excitement with constant, unstoppable enthusiasm and ongoing communication.

Bringing new members to a church congregation is like bringing in new members to any business or organization. It's critical that the folks who join an organization know right at the beginning how they fit into the big picture. They need to know what they will be taking a stand for, what it means, where it's going, who its customers are, who the competitors are, how they will deliver value to their customers and in what ways they will strive to create success for the individual, for the team member, and for the company. Having that high-visibility, opening day experience repeated time after time after time for new members of any organization is very critical.

When I think back to January 2002, when the new sanctuary was dedicated at Pinnacle Presbyterian Church, it was a wonderful, special day that we'll all remember for many years. Just as the original members received a beautiful glass ornament for Christmas trees, every member of the church in January 2002, received a memento that will be valued by each family for many years to come. That was a 'new opening day,' another significant step forward in the pursuit of excellence.

Great organizations are created because they nurture great people. They provide great opportunities for success for everyone. They constantly remind every person in the organization where they are and what their vision of the future is both from a communications stand point, from a visible behavior standpoint, and most importantly, from the sharing of success by the reaping of rewards for every member involved. So now we've had a great opening day and very visible success for all the vision and values work that has gone on in the past, and we are off and running.

In Chapter Seven we discuss the co-factor of momentum in any organization and how truly important it is to keep it going and stay focused. As we've said before, it is always critical to work backwards from the future vision of success.

PLANNING QUESTIONS

GREAT ANTICIPATION: NOW THAT WE'VE BUILT IT, WILL THEY COME?
Chapter Six

1. Will people come? _____
   Who will come? _____
   How many? _____
   How will they respond? _____
   Will their needs be met? _____
   Will they come back? _____

2. Picture your product/service five years from now. Working backwards from the future to the present, outline the steps necessary to get you there.

   _____
   _____
   _____
   _____
   What has to happen? _____

3. How will you create and advertise your opening day? _____

   _____
   Are you prepared for long days? _____
   Much stress? _____
   And great satisfaction? _____

4. How will you work toward your goals and what kind of team will be essential to success? _____

5. Will you be prepared to evolve with the entire organization? _____

   _____

6. You can't run around putting out fires, but you can set goals and control the growth process. How? _____
Will you build processes all the way through the organization? _____
_____
Which processes have you enjoyed being part of? _____
_____

7. How will you collectively celebrate achievements? _____
Can you recreate an "opening day" celebration time after time for new customers and employees? _____

8. How will you elevate, inspire, and motivate people? _____
_____
_____
_____

9. Leadership requires commitment; are you ready to make it? _____
_____
_____
_____

7

God Is in the Details— and So Are Great Leaders

LARRY

For those with minimal experience in the life of an organized church, know this: it is very much an event-driven phenomenon. In Pinnacle's formative years a defining event in Fall 1995 was the grand opening of the preschool. It triggered vigorous momentum in church growth despite its modest beginning with just sixteen students. Yet we are frequently reminded that one great teacher began with only twelve.

Next we look at how to:

- Continue in the right spirit.

- Make big transitions with grace.

- Break through the plateaus.

- Celebrate wins.

Even before the school opened, the classrooms were too small to accommodate the expected demand. Although the classroom building was only a year old, a decision was made to remove two partitions between the classrooms in order to enlarge them. It was a rare and stunning realization: that this or any church session (local board) was willing to take such a 'dramatic action' in less than a year of having opened the classrooms—and with such great pride of accomplishment.

Flexibility and adaptability were key contributing factors. Many churches would not have been willing to take such a significant step of making radical design changes on rooms so recently constructed. The reaction would have been, "What? You can't be serious!" Yet Pinnacle was constantly seeking to improve everything—and to do it all with a spirit of adaptability, flexibility, and excellence. Indeed, an underlying assumption about all of the space on the campus was that any of it could be shared and used for multi-purposes. Even the "sacred" space of the chapel was used by the local real estate companies for their introduction to weekly drive-by visits to new listings. Homeowners also used this space for annual meetings.

In addition to flexibility and adaptability, we practiced 'up close and personal' ownership of detail. For example, Janet Arbesman, the student intern preschool director made it a personal point to ensure that the sunshade over the preschool playground equipment sloped the same way as the roof of the adjacent classrooms. Such attention to detail was part of the larger planning process for all of the facilities of the church campus—even to the landscaping. We found it a simple thing to manage the tension between unwavering attention to detail and the need for flexibility, because our higher aim was and is a quality of experience and quality of appearance.

The preschool was an important part of the church's mission to serve the immediate community as well as to help families with a clear and present need. North Scottsdale is one of the wealthiest communities in the United States, but behind the gated walls of the residential communities and in the high-end, custom homes in the church's neighborhood are families in need. They have made such large financial commitments to buy their homes and decorate them with elegant furnishings that they have very little cash available on which to live. It is not unusual to have families in the preschool whose monthly mortgage payments are in a five-figure range seek scholarship assistance! Nor are sin and suffering kept at bay by guard gates—it's a fact of the human condition and has nothing to do with wealth or poverty. The mission field of this congregation is not limited to a third-world nation but in the immediate neighborhood where new parents appreciate an excellent preschool for their children. For the same reasons, the church gives sensitive pastoral care to adults suffering from illnesses, loneliness, and personal losses.

In the spirit of excellence, the preschool achieved accreditation with the National Association for the Education of Young Children (NAEYC) in its second year of operation. Such accreditation is very difficult to attain, and less than five per cent of the preschools in the nation, accredited by the NAEYC blue-ribbon organization. Part of the accreditation process was a form of benchmarking which took us to other suburban preschools to observe their best and weakest points.

Again, building an organization involves attention to countless, continuous details—and thank God the right people were willing to help at the right time. For instance, in the shared classroom space between the preschool and the church's Sunday School, Janet asked a church couple to help out each Friday afternoon—to come to the five preschool classrooms and convert them from the preschool-furniture configuration to the Sunday School configuration. This precious volunteer couple worked every Friday afternoon for nearly two years at this much-appreciated task. The Sunday School teachers would then rearrange the rooms at the end of their Sunday use into preschool readiness. Yes, God is in the details—like these and many others.

This sharing of space was a unique concept in a neighborhood where 'sharing' is not held in high esteem! Typically, children don't even share bedrooms or bathrooms. The more common *modus operandi* is 'what's mine is mine and yours is yours.'

Growth momentum continued to be energized by higher student enrollment and expansion. It also was experienced when a suggestion was made to give any preschool parent who would teach Sunday School a 10% discount on preschool tuition. This, too, was a unique concept that helped to increase the possibility of a parent volunteering to assist the Church Schoolteachers without breaking the preschool budget.

JERRE

You're right, and we've said this before. People will flow with the momentum when they sense they are a part of something greater—an environment of purpose, vision and energy. They seem to know, in most cases, that it's important to take a position and pitch in to help. One of the most conspicuous successes we've been blessed to have is momentum, momentum, and more momentum. Last year it was huge, with 160 new members. To keep something like this growing for 13 years is amazing.

LARRY

We have discussed the attention to detail that builds success. I also believe that it's the attention to detail that builds momentum. A person can't exploit the Spirit of God and say, "Got a minute? Great. We need to leverage your omnipotence." Or can we? Let's think about that. One can create the milieu in which God's Spirit may be more readily recognized and affirmed.

The very act of preparation has everything to do with giving attention to detail. One of the lessons I learned so clearly while on the college debate team was the value of being highly prepared. The more I prepared, the better the chances I would win the debate. The more I prepare the church situation, whether it is in worship, education, or administration, the greater the possibilities that someone will leave that experience saying, "Wow, that was great! The Spirit of God was in that place." Preparation is also vitally important in keeping focused on the goals of the church, and empowering others to help achieve them.

It changed my entire approach to ministry. I know all about that crazy business of running around trying to put out fires. Part of it was my need to please people. While I often still do that, I'm not as compulsive as I was. I've learned to have a Teflon skin. It goes with leadership. The toughest part for me to learn is I can't please everyone. I have to set my goals, explain them, and go with them. Some people will go with you and some won't. Some will move to where you want to go and some won't.

JERRE

One of the boards that my son, Jay, serves on is really wrestling with the CEO who got the company through the startup and now needs to change management styles. I found myself trying to help Jay find the right way to drive success for everyone involved. When I asked what was going on, Jay told me the CEO was holding on tight to every issue and decision. He just couldn't let go and trust others around him.

That happens to many people, leaders especially, and it's probably the single point that over time shapes a company's success. I can remember when I was physically and emotionally tired, and I had a tough time playing Mr. Teflon. When your defenses slip from fatigue, it's a challenge you must master. You need to stay fit and focused.

A former teacher I know, George Orlion, said, "If you're not careful, you'll find yourself with a bunch of monkeys running around your office, and you'll have to keep feeding them bananas all the time." It's so true. Part of the reason it's so important for leaders to keep themselves physically and mentally fit is when you get tired you lose your Teflon. When that happens, you lose your ability to lead.

LARRY

You lose not only your ability to lead, but you lose your ability to care. I tell people they need to take care of themselves or they won't have anything to give when they're really needed. It's true of leaders. If they don't take care of themselves, they won't be able to lead or care for others.

JERRE

It's true. I can think of people who worked for me, who got tired—and it shows.

A lot of times over the years people have asked me, "How can you be such a successful leader and be so nice?" I say they aren't separate things but one and the same. Good leaders absolutely do care about their people. Yet they don't allow those who detract to remain in leadership or high visibility.

I was thinking of David Kerns, retired CEO of Xerox. He took the helm at Xerox when they were a disaster 20 years ago. Remember when they were getting killed by Japanese companies because of their poor quality? He had worked his way up in Xerox and one day he finally became CEO. David took them down to the bottom and brought them up. It was really the first example of a true leadership change that used quality standards as the driver. Moreover, he did it when he had cancer in his nasal passages that caused his eyes to tear. He had the mental stress of this affliction along with problems in the struggling company. He conquered both—staying fit and facing the challenges. That's a leader.

After retiring he became the assistant Secretary of Education under President George Bush. The reason I mention this is he has done wonderful things for education. He always cared a lot about people and he showed it. He was told as an executive he would never be allowed to be Secretary of Education, but "would he mind being the assistant?" Here's a guy who has been CEO, who was tremendously respected, and he did it. He's a guy who lived through incredible headwinds and came through it all.

Work Out in Your 'Inner Fitness' Center

LARRY

I wonder what carried him through it? And, in the same way, what has carried you through the difficult times—when you've gone through them? I'm sure that in your years of leading large corporations, you must have devised ways to keep mentally fit and sustain your personal momentum.

JERRE

Two things always: first, a firm belief in God. Second, you have to forget yesterday and focus on tomorrow. I have a fundamental belief that I can't change what's happened. I can only work on the future. I really believe that God will help you get done what needs to get done. No matter how bad things are, it will work out. The hard part is realizing it may not work out the way I want it. In any case, I ground my energy in the two points of confidence I just mentioned. They are the foundation of my own 'inner fitness center'—and they are as important to me as physical fitness.

LARRY

Recently I heard a great line: "It's easier to ride the horse if you're going in the same direction as the horse." At times the corporation is not going in the direction you want it to and know it needs to, but it will be okay in spite of the fact you can't get the reins and get it turned around by yourself. To keep the momentum going, the leader often will need to convey a sense of urgency in addition to the details. And, always keep a radiant light aimed on the guiding vision.

JERRE

An example from MD On-Line comes to mind. Part of the reason Bill Bartzak is enjoying success now is that he's always stuck tenaciously to the vision he set out six years ago. He's been focused on the things he was going to do to make it better and better. At a recent board meeting, he told us that the CEO of the company, who wants to buy them, could not believe how Bill and his team can install his system in any office in the country without a physical presence. It blew him away. It's because Bill worked so hard on the system. He realized what a competitive advantage he'd have. He had carefully worked out the details—exactly to your point.

It's an art. They've got it down to where they can install a whole system in thirty minutes. I think the trick you pulled off here that makes a huge difference is your tenacious attention to details. Yet as growth continues you've had to shift more and more managing success through others. You don't lose the management of details, but you have brought it up two or three levels—and you have to sustain your personal energy to stay focused on executing those details—again, the inner fitness program.

LARRY

The inclination when you are treading through unfamiliar territory is to fall into a comfort zone populated by all the details you've been doing. What you're saying is we need to take the next step up, and attend to the details of the next level of management. That's the stage we're in.

JERRE

Absolutely. When we talked about the change from the chapel worship space to the new sanctuary, it was really taking a huge step forward. A company I serve as chairman of the board has three divisional presidents. One of them is a wonderful guy, but I don't know if he's going to be able to do what we've just been talking about. He's just been driving all the people who work for him crazy. Any time there's a problem he bypasses them and digs for the numbers. I told him the details he needs to focus on today is not what's wrong with the operation in Europe, but whether he has the right person in that job. If he doesn't, then what is he going to do about it? Aspiring leaders need to focus on details—like getting the right people in place, because those details are going to make you more successful.

LARRY

As you add staff, it's critical to help them be able to do this. One of the great things leaders can contribute is radiating light for others to see in, to focus in, and to work in.

Great Leaders Create New Spaces, New Opportunities, and Learn to Make Big Transitions with Grace

JERRE

I agree. And the light of leadership comes from a continuous entrepreneurialism in outlook—always looking for and fascinated by emerging opportunities. It's critical in a growing business that entrepreneurs never lose the entrepreneurial spirit. The natural entrepreneur must focus on bringing into existence new things, new spaces and new opportunities for those around him. The challenge is to guide your people into managing details that you once managed from sheer necessity.

This is the challenge of a great leader—an entrepreneur who knows how to manage details—yet is capable of rising, maturing, and teaching—reaching greater levels of achievement as he shows others how to replicate his leading ways.

The greatest leaders are mega-teachers, who know when it's time—the right time to let go—to move on and turn over the daily execution to people who themselves have risen to new heights. Like the singular and great figures of the Bible—the great leaders ascend into new realms of ever-greater vision and deeper, almost epic levels of responsibility. To some they may seem to suddenly vanish in the clouds—yet they are as focused and as active as ever—just in new, less-traveled spaces.

LARRY

Pinnacle church gained tremendous momentum after the preschool opened. Soon after that, the church acquired an additional five acres of land that triggered a new planning process for the addition of more parking spaces, an 8000 square foot Fellowship Hall building and a Memorial Garden. In the late '90's the world was being drawn into much turmoil. A bomber's explosion marred the opening of the 1996 Summer Olympics in Atlanta. A year later Hong Kong reverted to the Chinese mainland. The deaths of Princess Diana and Mother Teresa were in the news—yet the north Scottsdale area continued to experience additional rapid growth and expansion, seemingly untouched by the tragedies of the world beyond it. Driven by the mounting financial success of the high-tech market, the neighborhood kept on growing. And it took the church with it.

JERRE

When I look back over the path you took as CEO of Pinnacle, I see the many practices and special events that gave the church the successes we've gained. As we look forward, the fundamentals we've put in place will make our success continue.

I recently spoke with Bill Bartzak. He had just signed the largest contract of his career. About three years ago the company offering him the contract had tried to sweep him up and buy the company. Bill said no. It was so neat. He's now at the bridge.

LARRY

Does he realize that?

JERRE

Yes, he does. Not consciously. I reminded him. He asked me if I remembered when I told him it would take longer than he thought. He found it did take longer. Our discussion centered around: "Here are the things we've done and here's where we'll be in two or three years." He's come a long way—and he stuck it out. He transitioned through the tough times. You've already made the transition at Pinnacle.

LARRY

Recently I spoke with the session about the need for synergy in small groups. Each of the elders and deacons needed to have that happen. I could tell by the looks on their faces that either they weren't getting it, or that they still felt the loss of the chapel. I spoke about the synergy that was there because of the closeness, the children, the music, and friendliness.

I believe this kind of synergy is a small group phenomenon. We'll never have that in the large open sanctuary no matter how good the preaching, music, or children. So the synergy has to take place in small closely-woven groups. I see it in our Habitat for Humanity volunteers. I see it in the Amigos, a social/service group in the church. I'm not sure they understood. I think it has to be repeated over and over in other formats.

JERRE

It's about communication. As Kathleen Janson, a woman who once worked for me, said, "The only time you've ever said something often enough is when you can go any place and ask them and they can repeat it back to you." It's such a key point we need to do it a dozen ways over and over and over.

LARRY

As we grow from 1,000 to 1,500 in the next few years, I will become pastor to the staff, elders, and deacons. The staff, in effect, will become middle managers. In the process my role changes. That can be tough.

One of our church members tells the story of leaving his church in Edina, Minnesota. His father died and the minister never called or spoke with them about it. He felt as if the minister didn't care. This member doesn't want our church to grow—because he liked the small congregation relationships and the intimacy between the pastor and the smaller church. He likes it when the minister is in close touch with the individuals and events happening around him. I don't know how that fits in business. It's a challenge because you can't just be the pastor to the staff, but you have to be available to the general public. You have to be willing to make the calls and do the pastoral care.

JERRE

It's tough because you have been there from the beginning. If a new person were in that chair, they would not relate back to you in that way. The neat part is being able to reach through that and keep the continuity going. Because you were there, it's a huge difference.

When I joined Ingram Micro as CEO we were a fair sized company at $8 billion in annual sales, but it was mostly domestic. So, I would go to every Monday morning's US staff meeting of the top 40 people. I always sat in the back of the room. If they asked me something, I'd comment. I used that as a platform every now and then when there was something critical to communicate. Three years later, as we grew we also had added a $5 billion Asia Pacific regional sales team and $8 billion in the European Region. Our growth was explosive, and guess what happened: I got crucified. I heard people say, "You don't care about us anymore. You don't spend time with us." So I went back and said Sonat Datta is the North American president now. Sonat had a Mexican and a Canadian president reporting to him. He's become "the man" so to speak for the North American Region. And he's at the top of an international corporation. It doesn't mean you can't e-mail or call me. It just means that I will be in many more places than in the past.

LARRY

I see the same dynamic in the church. People say, "You don't come to every Amigos (a social group in the church) meeting anymore!" I tell them I cannot go to every church function any more. It's okay. It doesn't mean I don't care. Every time the church doors are open I can't be at every function.

JERRE

I would also encourage you to speak to the elders about that issue. They have to help take on that activity. That's a way to get the message back to these different groups that things are working in new ways. You've got to do that. Having lived through that at

Ingram Micro, I know exactly what you're experiencing. It takes a year or two. It takes time for parishioners to know there are other people there who can do just as well.

I told Kent Foster when he was hired, here are some of the disadvantages—but there are some unique advantages. One of the great ones is you're not going to be as connected as I am. He asked, "What do you mean?" I told him he'd be able to use the platform he wanted to get the messages to them. Kent's was a live video conference every month. You won't get trapped because they've never seen you there.

Your platform, Larry, is Sunday morning. I've thought about it quite a bit. It will be different with another full-time associate pastor.

The Leadership Journey Includes Plateaus, Transitions and Successes

LARRY

Pinnacle did have some problems but the reality is they were quite manageable. We were so fortunate. To some extent the plateaus were the biggest ones and the financial hurdles never really existed because we started out rent-free for five years and Valley was paying my compensation. We ended up having excess revenues every year. This is the first year cash flow has been a problem.

We had $80,000 surplus at the beginning of the first year.

There have been many transitions and bridges Pinnacle Presbyterian has crossed during its short existence. One of them was the acquisition of the third five acres. It gave us the first opportunity to consider additional parking. We only had 70 parking spaces and that was inadequate even for the chapel. We understood we could not grow if we didn't have adequate parking space.

Another early change was when Janet Arbesman, the associate pastor, left to get her Ph.D. and Duane Holloran, Ph.D., replaced her.

JERRE

We became personally active during that period. We left the first Sunday morning with the feeling this was a great group of people. You were on vacation that Sunday, so we decided to wait...until the "real" pastor would show up. We enjoyed the people and experience so much. Later, when Duane arrived you could almost feel the exponential step. You split the responsibilities almost evenly, and the positive feeling between the two of you was evident.

LARRY

We became competitive in a friendly way. It was like playing a golf game. Duane and I had known each other for 20 years and I'd been president of his board of directors. We knew each other well enough that we could compete in the pulpit and in worship, yet we were completely supportive of each other. That chemistry effervesced.

JERRE

It was great. And then I remember the real excitement that came when we got the books in the new sanctuary, "Come Grow with Us." In 1999, I believe. You could feel how exciting everything was.

The next huge burst of momentum came from the future vision of the church that was so clearly communicated. We could see the layout of everything going forward. From our standpoint, the Memorial Garden was critical because it represented a very permanent place.

LARRY

By implication it said, "We are going to be here." We built the Memorial Garden two or three years before the new sanctuary. It came with the Fellowship Hall and additional parking spaces. I suggested and encouraged the Memorial Garden because I saw it as a source of income for the church. It hasn't happened to the degree I thought it would. Repository site purchases have been slower than anticipated.

JERRE

I was also thinking that the completion of Fellowship Hall was another big step forward. Two things come to mind. First was the fall 'Round-up.' Many people were there and we all felt a wonderful presence. Then, I recall the first Christmas in there. It was incredibly special. You've got to keep that momentum going. When I think about things you've done here—as compared to what businesses do,it comes down to having those 'kickers' to keep things going.

LARRY

They also help to break through the plateaus. When we contemplated major building projects and program development, the finance committee would always ask me if we were biting off more than we could chew. I kept saying to them, "Giving begets giving." It will not hurt the other programs; if anything it will enhance it.

JERRE

You did have problems, but because of what we just said, it kept it going. Actually, momentum creates momentum. That's what's happened almost every year.

LARRY

In chapter six, I wrote about getting hung up on the plateau of 70 members and how it seemed we couldn't get past it in order to charter. The event that broke it was the Sunday that Meredyth and I announced we were putting our home on the market and were going to move out here. The congregation broke out in applause. I was dumbfounded. I thought: "Why are they applauding?"

In the next few months those 70 people went out and found 30 more. I realized I was asking them to make a commitment when they thought I had not. Buying a house was obviously a sign of our commitment. They then responded with a commitment to the marriage. Once I made that major, visible commitment, things took off. Here I was asking them to make a commitment when they felt I hadn't. I was surprised at the impact it had on my leadership.

JERRE

The house decision was probably the first event kicker. As we get into this discussion we need to think about those six or seven steps that were critical. How you handle the plateaus is critical.

LARRY

Gaining that momentum, Pinnacle Presbyterian Church also grew in membership, programming, and staff. In 2001, our organization was recognized as the 33rd fastest-growing church in the United States. With a major gift from one of its families, the last five-acre parcel was acquired, which completed the geographic master plan of twenty acres for the church campus.

The staff also grew, with a full time associate pastor added; a full time director of church education, and a ten million-dollar capital fund drive initiated in 1999 to build five more classrooms, a central administration complex, and a 12,000 square foot sanctuary with a seating capacity for 850 persons. Simultaneously, the church was to build the first of six annual 'Habitat for Humanity' houses in the Phoenix area, while increasing its benevolent financial contributions in direct proportion to its growing annual income.

The tenth anniversary soon arrived in 1999, and as the local Arizona Diamondbacks made it to the playoffs, the church was quietly celebrating its first decade of life. That celebration was highlighted with four million dollars committed from two families to launch the capital funds drive for the new facilities. Talk about momentum! Once again, the members and friends of the church stepped up to the plate to make significant contributions to our growing church.

But the turmoil of the world was soon to take its effect on the high tech economy and that was signaled with the tragic earth shaking events of September 11, 2001.

JERRE

As I think back on each of the organizations over the years that I've been part of or studied, keeping momentum, keeping things happening, and having targets for people to be measured against is critical. Then, finding ways to help them celebrate their wins is also important in any organization. Larry has done an outstanding job of that with staff at Pinnacle Presbyterian. We've always had great successes, great events, and great things to celebrate.

When I think of the three companies we've been talking about I think of each of them in a different way as to momentum. When Scott and his team at GolfLogix signed their agreement for Canada and Europe, it gave them tremendous momentum. They received wonderful recognition when Pebble Beach began installing their system. It was a huge step forward in momentum.

In Chapter Eight we'll talk about the challenges that have been created because of the great momentum happening at GolfLogix.

Bill Bartzak, CEO at MD On-line, is an ongoing success story today because he stayed so focused on creating a momentum in his industry. Although it took years to see it come to fruition, today the momentum there is the greatest indication of momentum I've seen in an organization in many years.

Today, Bill is spending an amazing amount of his time listening to new customers who have just installed MD On-Line—and is using his methodology and model across the board. He succeeds every time. Why? Because he provides the best service, he is the most effective in his field, and he's proven over time it is a great way to meet or exceed customer needs.

When I look at WorkWell today, I see two of the executives, George Carpenter and Mitch Hill, anticipating a significant merger. This will create tremendous momentum for their organization. Even to be working toward such a great success step gives great momentum to WorkWell. Why? They set out a vision, they have executed against that vision, and they are about to see great success as a result of it.

When I think of different organizations I've known over time, certainly the last one, Ingram Micro, where we tripled in head count around the world in a three-year period, and more than tripled our revenue, it was because we stayed very focused on our vision. We worked backwards from the future, and did a better job of taking care of our customers than our competitors.

We also worked hard to provide ongoing information inside the organization, so people could see how much fun it was to win. Winning happens in all organizations that follow these principles and practices— whether they are for-profit or non-profit, like Pinnacle Presbyterian. It means so much to see new people come join us, and the thrill of helping them join the growing family of success. Winning at our church means providing environments for great music, wonderful children's programs, reaching out into the community, state, nation, and in fact into the world. Being part of a winning organization has a way of replicating itself in people's lives—and their relationships—and can affect people and events across the world.

As we move to our next and final chapter called "Shining the Light to Create a Clear Line of Sight," it's really about building a bridge from our success—that began 15 years ago, and extends into the future, a very bright future. It tells of accepting the challenges, focusing the priorities, keeping the resources, looking forward always with the intent of meeting or exceeding that vision that we set out and we continue to renew time after time.

PLANNING QUESTIONS

God is in the Details: and So Are Great Leaders
Chapter Seven

1. How will you continue the mission and vision of your start-up days?

   _____

   _____

   _____

   _____

2. As the company organization grows how will you gracefully make big transitions to a different style of management? _____

   _____

   _____

3. As customers' needs shift how will you be flexible and adaptable while maintaining your mission and vision? _____

   _____

   _____

4. How will you make plans to take care of yourself as you care for others?

   _____

   _____

5. What carries you through times of stress? _____

   _____

   What sustains you in the face of great obstacles? _____

   _____

   _____

8

SHINING THE LIGHT TO CREATE CLEAR LINE OF SIGHT

LARRY

I grew up in a small southeastern Ohio village. It was a very Norman Rockwell kind of atmosphere, and the pace was slower—it was the 1950s. At that time my father owned and operated a two-pump service station in a neighboring town. I started working there at twelve, pumping gas (at 24 cents a gallon), cleaning windshields that I could barely reach, checking air in the tires, and generally helping wherever Dad needed me (for 50 cents an hour, which was pretty good for those times).

Dad was typically frustrated with me because my personal interest in and aptitude for mechanical tools or auto repair was marginal. I preferred socializing with customers, asking about their lives and listening to their jokes. In fact, the shallow banter of a garage accessorized with automotive parts was often an exercise in adolescent sex education.

Unfortunately, I had no talent for the kind of technical assistance Dad needed. But there was one task I could do, and I became quite adept at it: I was often called upon to hold the light while he was under the hood or beneath a vehicle, making repairs.

Dad used a mechanic's droplight to work on the cars hoisted into the air to service them from the chassis. He often needed me to hold the light at just the right angle, which enabled him to see the project under repair more clearly. I would dutifully hold it while adjusting the angle per his instruction. Sometimes, this seemed to go on for long periods until my arm would ache and I'd have to shift hands and reposition. I learned the value of aiming the beam of light to a precise point and angle so that Dad's line-of-sight was perfect for the task.

Holding the light occurred frequently beyond the service station as well. My father believed in on-site calls, i.e., visiting customer homes or the roadside, fixing a flat tire and other types of customer service, on the spot exactly where needed. It seemed like these calls most often happened after dusk had settled, when darkness was falling on the hills and narrow roads of eastern Ohio. He'd take me with him on those late calls, and sure enough, my assignment was to hold the light.

In some instances it was a large flashlight which he kept in the car for emergency use. Remember those metal, silver-handled models they used to make? I'd help locate the wheel lugs and nuts as he'd take off a tire to change it. It was very important to keep that light focused on the right spot as he strained and yanked to loosen the nuts and remove the wheel. A few years later, after getting my driver's license, he'd send me by myself to do a tire repair. Sure, I could do it. However, I could never do the repair as quickly or with the ease and pace Dad could. I was much better at just holding the light.

This practice was also true at home where my mechanical skills were relegated to pulling the starting rope on an old rotary, orange Jacobson lawn mower that would never start without a battle. Having nearly an acre of grass to mow, each week I came to dread these days as the stupid mower rarely started. I'd pull the rope until my arm went numb, and unfailingly, would have to wait for Dad to come home for supper. Then, in the shadows of our dimly lit basement, I'd hold the flashlight for him once again while he made some carburetor adjustment or other modification to get the lawn mower going.

Afterward I'd sit there feeling like a failure while he'd rush around at high speed behind the mower trying to cut the grass as the sun set. Nonetheless, I became a virtuoso at the fine art of flashlight and droplight management. I soon acquired recognition for my mastery of lightman-ship—and folks would talk about my characteristic skill. I took it at as a positive—I felt I knew best how to aim a light on a problem to be solved!

My light-shining role soon became a kind of family joke. "You need a flashlight? Call Larry." The family assumed that I couldn't do much to fix anything or put anything together, but I was great at holding the light, and shining it in such a way that it helped to get the job done.

Years later, after my wedding, my young wife and I set out on a camping trip with another couple near a shore in New Jersey. I couldn't begin to put up our tent, but dutifully held the light while my wife and friends erected and stabilized it. Having provided my unique contribution of talent, I then slept peacefully.

During my younger years, however, I was pro-actively developing leadership skills. At sixteen, I was active in the church and elected Youth Moderator of the Wheeling Presbytery of the United Presbyterian Church of North America.

A few months later, at another election, I was chosen to be the Youth Moderator of the Ohio Synod. These two responsibilities were a delight! With my parent's permission, and often at their expense, I traveled from town to town in Ohio.

I was part of a team of well-trained teenagers who went to various local churches to help them with the development of their youth ministry. My efforts were focused on public speaking and acting (in dramas in both the church and high school). I also became good at creating a guiding vision for local church youth programs. Later, I excelled in college debate—where the team activities revealed to me a whole new range of concepts pertaining to light.

This became a sort of personal theme—one of bringing light to the lives of people I knew and the organizations I joined. This more refined practice of light-bearing brought great personal satisfaction. For once, I was providing light because light was needed most—I wasn't just doing it because I didn't know which end of a wrench to hold!

I was learning a lesson in leadership—that a key part of it is the ability to direct the light for someone. A good leader knows that a radiant light must shine:

- To reveal the guiding vision for creating a better future.

- To illuminate its essential tenets, and share the potential results.

- To light the way across, through and around barriers and boundaries—to achieve the greater goal or meet the higher need despite obstructions.

- To provide a clear line of sight for processes, decisions, human resources, and evaluation.

- To bring details into bright focus for every undertaking or program.

The challenge of shining a light—envisioning—a successful future for Pinnacle Presbyterian Church—was rewarding. It provided a foreseeable and underlying hope for the many individuals on the steering committee. The scriptures say it well, "For the vision is for days yet to come." (Old Testament, Daniel 10:14)

The leadership light shines…into the future to illuminate possibilities…and into the present to illuminate realities—so that faced and managed, all things can lead to higher qualities of life. It also shows the way to promising personal relationships, for instance, when relocating families move into new residential developments.

The process of sharing an enlightened vision helped to create a gathering of people willing to work to affirm all that Pinnacle Presbyterian Church could be—a safe place to come to seek answers to one's questions regarding the scriptures, moral and ethical issues, and meaning in life. Time after time people responded to invitations to make a commitment to actively joining the Pinnacle community. Such commitments came when the participants perceived that belonging to this church would make a significant difference in their lives, as well as making an impact on North Scottsdale.

The quest began with hopeful, small, personal steps forward—acts of weekly volunteer support by members of the Valley Presbyterian Church. They helped set up chairs and transform a real estate office into space for worship. They established a well-structured volunteer system in the current church office. And over the years, people have stepped forward to become personally engaged in the life and ministry of the church in many practical helpful ways—as well as the more demanding fund-raising tasks.

They have gained a deep sense of ownership of the church's mission and ministry as they have committed their financial resources, time, and creative talents. An issue with which the church wrestles as it drives toward a powerful and exciting future is protecting and guiding its children in volunteer church school programs.

At the present time in the U.S. cultural milieu, the Roman Catholic organization is still reeling with scandals of child molestation—and the resulting cover-ups at higher judicatory levels. Such emotionally and spiritually devastating issues have caused churches nationwide of many denominations to put new restrictions in place in order to protect children, yet also protect the churches themselves from costly lawsuits.

To that end, the Pinnacle Presbyterian Church board is presently engaged in discerning appropriate safeguard measures to put into place without undermining its message of openness and hospitality. We boldly proclaim that our church is a safe place to bring one's children but also one's doubts, fears and questions. The church leadership needs to direct the living light of the Word on specific issues as well as the broader vision and mission of the greater church—while instilling confidence and defeating fear and negativity with credible affirmations and demonstrations of the reality of Christ's living leadership.

With such critical moral, civil and spiritual issues confronting the church, the need for visible leadership and higher intelligence has become a top priority. The vision, scope and intelligence in which decisions are made by the board, committees, and staff is vital to the church's immediate future. The decision-making process must seek always to uphold the trust of its leaders, those responsible for affecting lives throughout the church system, and ensure that the results are congruent with the choices of those responsible for the decisions. If a decision is made to spend money on an agreed-upon program, then that decision must be honored by all the responsible parties. Otherwise, trust is broken in the process. It's the responsibility of leadership to focus a light on this challenge, regardless of the consequences.

The light must be directed as well in developing ways of evaluating programs and profits. For a non-profit organization, leadership will always need to consider answers to these traditional questions:

- For whom is the program aimed?

- Who will benefit from the program and how?

- What will it cost?

- Who will staff it?

- When will it occur?

- What will be the outcome?
- How will it be evaluated?

In the chapel at Pinnacle Presbyterian Church visitors can see a clear message in its creatively fashioned windows—a message of limitless hope. It echoes the truths found in the opening verses of the Gospel of John, "What has come into being in Christ was life, and the life was the light of all people. The light shines in the darkness, and the darkness has not overcome it." (New Testament, John 1: 4–5)

In the wildly complex panorama of daily life across the globe, we see the dynamic contrasts of both beautiful light and terrifying darkness. Television has become a living portal into the experiences of human lives in a thousand places, cultures, and countries. We see the beauty in human relationships and vast, picturesque landscapes. Yet we also see devastation brought on by terrorism and ignorance.

Never before in history has so much been at stake. People cry out for transforming leadership—for an illuminating, enlightened leadership capable of holding up the Living Light for those in search of a meaningful future. Even in the free world, shadows of many kinds stalk those who seek a better life—a transforming light.

Pinnacle Presbyterian Church is prepared to respond to such a challenge so that it can shine a light on the love of God that will not let us go, will not let us down, and will not let us off the hook of personal responsibility.

JERRE

Holding and shining the light is truly a wonderful way of thinking about leadership, which requires vision, clarity, and illumination. It works in business and in spiritual experience—where opening people's eyes to ways they can become more successful must become a top priority. When Larry says, "I am learning that leadership is the ability to hold the light for some-one...that shining the light is creating a future," he describes perfectly what great leaders do to create great success.

As we look forward into the future of each of the business organizations we've talked about, it's an exciting time. They have in fact made the transition that Larry and his team have accomplished. They've grown from startup to maturity, much like Pinnacle's development—becoming flourishing organizations that offer so much for so many.

Pinnacle Church has met or exceeded its original goals set out more than 13 years ago—and now looks to expand even more. For example, they aspire to one day provide over 50% of their annual income to missions throughout the country and world. And they expect to do this while creating and continuing to support a wonderful community center for music, programs, worship, and retreats that would allow many organizations to come and share together.

MD On-Line is now flourishing and Bill Bartzak is still leading. His organization is now recognized and his company is well known in their industry. He has new challenges of growth, new challenges that he meets each and every day as he continues to execute toward perfection, meeting the needs of current and future customers. Bill's organization has moved through an incredible series of difficult events and now is poised to become an outstanding, profitable, customer-focused company working forward as a model into the future, providing tools for all the medical industry for years to come.

Scott and his team at GolfLogix are faced with a new challenge. They are growing so rapidly and the demand is so high that they need to borrow short-term funds to be able to keep the needs of the organization going. They've created success in a very short time—and they are committed to exceeding the expectations of everyone by pursuing excellence.

Frankly, WorkWell is fascinating. The vision that Lance and Cory started more than five years ago has recently grown into success by becoming two organizations—both with great and promising futures. They have been successful by remembering and applying the critical elements of success: focusing on their key values, building a foundation based on those values, and creating meaningful requirements for their people—who are measured by the success of their customers.

Thus far in this book we've talked about four wonderful start-ups all led by entrepreneurs. Primarily we've focused on Larry Corbett, who has become an outstanding CEO, minister, pastor, and supporter for countless people—shining a bright light to create a clear line of sight.

Scott and his team at GolfLogix will be recognized in two or three years as the company that provides the best tools to help golfers all over the world improve their game. Bill Bartzak and his team today are recognized as the single most effective internet system available to the medical industry to reduce bureaucracy, improve cost control, and most importantly meet the needs of medical customers quickly. Lance and Cory's WorkWell will be helping more and more companies achieve financial health by smartly resolving work-injury problems.

It's interesting to look back and think about the church that Larry and others created as a startup. Now they are on a bridge to 2000 members—a pattern of successful growth. They have a program that creates wonderful opportunities for hundreds of children throughout the north Scottsdale area. And it's more than a church—it has become a total environment for a healing spiritual experience, with effervescent worship and music that will attract people throughout Phoenix for years to come.

Significantly, this is a church that has been built by the raising up of a boundless Light—for limitless success where people, one at a time, can discover a clearer line of sight to the wonderful possibilities they have been given by their Creator.

It is a privilege to share the insights I have gathered as a chief executive officer of leading companies across many industries. The complex realities of business at every level require an uncommon commitment to illumination—to asking the right questions, exposing the realities of every situation, and of direct-ing the force and energy of light to create an environ-ment of success. It's a fitting analogy—the light of leadership creates clear line of sight—to our cus-tomers, to our responsibilities, to our future—and to each needed next step it takes to get there.

And, finally, I look forward to supporting Larry and the church in the future. Larry has closed his remarks appropriately. I join him by affirming that Pinnacle Presbyterian Church is poised to respond to the chal-lenge—so they can shine a light on the love of God that will not let us go, will not let us down, and will not let us off the hook of personal responsibility. We have done our best in these pages to shine the light for you.

PLANNING QUESTIONS

Shining the Light to Create Clear Line of Sight
Chapter Eight

1. A key lesson in leadership is the ability to direct the light for someone —
   to reveal the guiding vision for creating a better future;
   to illuminate its essential tenets,
   and share the potential results;
   to light the way across, through and around barriers and boundaries;
   achieve the greater goal or meet the higher need despite obstructions;
   to provide a clear line of sight for processes, decisions, human resources,
   and evaluation;
   to bring details into bright focus for every undertaking or program.

   With this awareness how do you see yourself providing leadership for
   your vision? _____
   What will it cost, personally as well as financially? _____
   _____
   What will be the rewards? _____
   _____